Date Due

CHANGE IN THE VILLAGE

CHANGE IN THE VILLAGE

by

GEORGE BOURNE, *1863–1927*

AUGUSTUS M. KELLEY · PUBLISHERS

NEW YORK 1969

First published 1912
Reprinted 1920, 1927, 1935
This Edition, reset, 1955
Reprinted 1959

All rights reserved

First published in the United States by
Augustus M. Kelley · Publishers
New York, New York 10001
SBN 678 08001 1

Library of Congress Catalogue Card Number
75-86314

Printed in Great Britain

TO
MY SISTERS

CONTENTS

I

II

THE PRESENT TIME

III

THE ALTERED CIRCUMSTANCES

IV

THE RESULTING NEEDS

V

INTRODUCTION

By Geoffrey Grigson

THIS is a book to read slowly and deliberately, in the way it was written. George Bourne, or, to give him his proper name, George Sturt, lived a neighbour of the poor, as their employer and friend, who studied their ways and their society through most of his life. So *Change in the Village* was not a piece of sentimental or pastoral journalism, quickly thrown off. It was published when he was in his late forties, after years of enquiry. Always in earnest with his subject, always in earnest with words, the author, as one would guess, even if it had not been stated by his friend Arnold Bennett the novelist, found writing difficult and slow; the result is a well-constructed prose, cool and steady and deliberate, which does not flow into, and pass out of, the mind too quickly.

A few words about George Bourne will explain why he was equipped to write about village people. He was close to the labouring class, without belonging to it. On one side he was descended from the proprietors of a small country business (which he inherited) supplying the farmers' need, on the other side from the farmers themselves. It was his grandfather who had purchased the wheelwright's business at Farnham, in Surrey, in 1800; his father took over the business in 1865 and conducted it until 1884. But his father was not altogether so isolated in his country environment as his grandfather had been. He was not so much a fly immovable in amber. Already more influence of extraneous thought, more enquiry, were reaching into the countryside. The horizon was extending. In another of his books, *A Small Boy in the Sixties*, George Sturt—as I shall call him for the rest of this introduction—describes how the Sturts took their first holiday, how as a child he went to Bognor in 1874, the first time that he looked at the sea; and if not the first time that his mother had beheld it, no more than the second. He quotes an uncle exclaiming, " I can't think what you want to go away for!" years later, when any of his family asked for relaxation; but then his uncle had fitted " closely into the environing countryside," with an intimacy no longer so common to people of Sturt's generation (he was born in 1863). " I, for one," he adds, " have never been into the country in that intense way," and he implies, incidentally, that his grandfather, who acquired the business, would have thought business and shop insulted by the taking of a holiday.

Had Sturt fitted too closely into the environment of the Surrey countryside, he could never have seen it in such definition; had he been too separate, divorced from it by too great a distinction of class, he would have seen it without so much understanding. Time and circumstances combined with his talent and gave him the degree of closeness and detachment he required. He knew even then that he must work for his insight and information. He made his living for years in the family business (after a spell as a schoolmaster), yet he trained himself in freedom and observation—refusing, for example, to let himself walk with the self-regarding gait of a local businessman. His shop brought him into daily touch with workmen, though he detested the relationship of master and servant. Yet however close his study, even when he had moved out of his country town into a village (into the village of this book), he knew that he was willy-nilly of a different social species to the people he investigated and described. " If one could get down to understand village life!" he wrote to Arnold Bennett in 1898. " I have reached that initiatory stage in which one is convinced of ignorance. . . . It were almost as easy to write of the Chinese." One may guess how important and how fascinating the job became to him, from one small fact. The village he described in this book gave him his pen-name. It was The Bourne, and he became George " Bourne " for all except two of his series of books about countrymen and their society or their individuality.

The Bourne was his laboratory, yet there is nothing about *Change in the Village* of the sociological report or the statistical analysis. Sturt might view things, as we would say now, ecologically, studying what he called the " human fauna " of a " patch of England," he might have his serious topic, he might wish to investigate with accuracy, but he was a writer, he was a considerable artist, who worked always to make his writing connect more firmly and be more effective. He believed in the worth of man, of labouring man and labouring wife as he encountered them in his Surrey village; but he was always on sentry-go against falsity or an easy sentiment in himself, unsupported by evidence. He belonged to a period in which many people were concerned once again with what the poet Gerard Manley Hopkins called a " strong modern realism," giving George Crabbe as an earlier example. It was a realism at work in painting as well as literature, in Whistler's homage to Courbet and in the drawings of Charles Keene, as well as in Kipling, Hardy, and Hopkins himself, and then in the novels of Sturt's friend Arnold Bennett, many of which he read and criticized in manuscript. Sturt would not have mentioned Crabbe—at least, he had no poetry in him, not even a sad poetry like Crabbe's in his tales of Suffolk. But he did mention William Cobbett (also born and bred at Farnham), he did hold before himself the example of Cobbett, who had delineated, in prose unstilted and crisply defined, an earlier phase of rural transition. He admired also the forthright prose of Thoreau, that unfearing evangelist of proper living; and he sympathized with the Fabians, not feeling it God-ordained and immutable that the poor should always be poor and harassed. If he lacked Cobbett's passion, he was less hasty in his conclusions. If he lacked the delightful freshness of Thoreau (there is nothing so haunting in Sturt's prose as the green ponds of Walden), he also lacked Thoreau's eccentricity; and if he had Fabian sympathies, he kept inside the Fabian boundaries of gradualism and moderation. All was kept within such bounds. Sturt, the bachelor living with his sisters and painfully acquiring his art and his evidence, was a careful man—careful to make his case, with no desire for the barricades.

His case in this book was not difficult or abstruse. The more he studied his human fauna upon their patch of late Victorian or Edwardian England, the more he could see them bewildered in the slow phase of a revolution. In England as elsewhere in Europe, the unit of country life had for centuries been the village community with its lands, the community in its ancient shape of peasants sharing the hay meadows, the three great tillage fields cropped in rotation, and the rough land which afforded not only rough grazing but a score of the necessities of daily life, from kindling to bracken for bedding the cattle. Through four centuries there had been a gradual revolution to bring about a more efficient use of the land—the common land, which was newly divided, handed over to individual, independent control, and enclosed. A result was the creation of those poor landless labourers whose distress so moved the heart, so roused the indignation of Cobbett, and a hundred years later so engaged the critical and probing sympathies of George Sturt.

Once, Sturt declares, there had been a viable civilization of the countryside, a " living engine with a fly-wheel of tradition," a civilization of those peasants who had lived by a common environmental knowledge rather than by private judgments, who had " derived the necessities of life from the material and soil of their own countryside." This peasant tradition " permitted a man to hope for well-being without seeking to escape from his own class into some other." Sturt knew that this peasant civilization had gone for ever, in most of Great Britain. He was in no way one of those wistful writers who slew their heads around and gaze at the shining trees of Paradise. He did not want to restore what cannot be restored, and he preferred the possibility of something better. Meanwhile he looked at what there was to see. There were, of course (as there still are) fragments of the old compulsions, the old ways, the old values. Turner, the handyman of the village, so closely described in Chapter XV, who reminded Sturt of the older dispensation, is of a type surviving still in the villages, able to do many things from thatching to grafting or pruning, and impatient of owning to any master except himself. But Sturt was no collector of fragments or of country quaintness. Looking about him in the Surrey of 1912, he saw labouring men and women too often unhappy and worried, too often " low-spirited, mirthless and all but silent," a community of wage-earners whose living was no longer in their own hands and whose wages were too small. He observed in them an " ill-defined but chronic anxiety," from which few of the cottages were free for any length of time—" for though there is not much extreme destitution, a large number of the villagers live always on the brink of it; they have the fear of it always in sight."

He looked a little higher and there he saw the educated, the propertied, acting towards the uneducated and unpropertied without understanding. He saw the middle classes wanting to civilize the worker, to " do him good "—wanting, Sturt shrewdly decides, " to make him more like themselves, and yet keep him in his place of dependence and humiliation." The village had its policeman (always, as Sturt remarked, the lonely man of the parish) : it seemed he was there to keep his eye on those underneath in the interest of those above. Magistrates, to the working-man in the box and to his wife listening to the prosecution, seemed to represent the same interest. Coming to education, Sturt was not the only observer to have misgivings, to detect in public education a smell of misdirected charity to the lower orders. When he wrote, there had been more than twenty years of educational ferment, even revolution. Commissions had reported, reforms had been launched, local authorities had been given the power to provide evening classes, the Board of Education had been set up, and school-going had been made at last compulsory. The Elementary School Code of 1904 was informed by a new spirit—that working-class education was for the children and the whole community, that it was neither a charity nor an insurance policy taken out by the middle classes for their own safety. Sturt nevertheless contemplated the education which came to the village from outside, from the deliberations of men so much outside, and so much above, that they had no finger upon the " spontaneous movement of the village life;" and he was sceptical. He might still be sceptical to-day at a continued cleft between village life and village schooling.

It is indeed a virtue of his book that it makes one question complacencies and apparent axioms. It was, of course, an interim view that Sturt presented. " The old rural outlook of England," he declared, was dead : the rural English were " waiting for something new to take its place, for some new tradition to grow up amongst them "; they were " between two civilizations "—one had lapsed, the other had not yet come the way of the rural English. For all their honesty, patience, resignation and courage (on a family income that *might* approach twenty-four shillings a week), their condition was then, he thought, stagnant. Yet he detected symptoms of the great amelioration which has taken place between his time and ours, he saw already an infiltration of thinking and ideas.

Sturt's new rural civilization has to grow to maturity even now, though anyone who has known an English village through the last thirty or forty years, in the time since George Sturt's death in 1927, will admit both the changes and the amelioration, no matter what may be questioned in detail. Buses, bicycles, motor-bicycles and hard winter roads; easy access not only to work, but to towns and cinemas; more papers, more reading, more books from the County Library; the enjoyment of broadcasting, and of television as the H aerials

sprout on cottage and council house; the council houses themselves with their means of pleasanter living; holidays, with pay,
for those who in Sturt's time had no prospect of holiday as
long as they lived—such things indeed are making a new rural
civilization, less starved in emotion and in mind. A roughness and a savagery, which Sturt acknowledged, have gone.
With higher wages, in a Welfare State, anxieties and apathies
are diminished. So in many ways the hopes of this acute
observer nearly half a century ago have been fulfilled. Yet
Change in the Village is not to be read simply for facts, conclusions and surmises. It does reveal, fascinatingly, some of
the facts inside that sentimental haze which other writers have
spread around the cottages and around country living. But a
greater merit of the book is its sympathetic perception : it tells
us to look into situations, into men's lives, to pierce, if we can,
to that "spontaneous movement" of life, before we presume
to offer advice, to provide palliatives, to condemn or to praise.
It convicts our pride of its offence, teaches us, too, that sympathetic understanding is best reached by rejecting the tyranny of
accepted ideas, and by a scepticism, if as gentle, then as firm, as
that of George Sturt.

I

THE VILLAGE

I

THE VILLAGE

IF one were to be very strict, I suppose it would be wrong to give the name of " village " to the parish dealt with in these chapters, because your true village should have a sort of corporate history of its own, and this one can boast nothing of the kind. It clusters round no central green; no squire ever lived in it; until some thirty years ago it was without a resident parson; its church is not half a century old. Nor are there here, in the shape of patriarchal fields, or shady lanes, or venerable homesteads, any of those features that testify to the immemorial antiquity of real villages as the homes of men; and this for a very simple reason. In the days when real villages were growing, our valley could not have supported a quite self-contained community : it was, in fact, nothing but a part of the wide rolling heath-country—the " common," or " waste," belonging to the town which lies northwards, in a more fertile valley of its own. Here, there was no fertility. Deep down in the hollow a stream, which runs dry every summer, had prepared a strip of soil just worth reclaiming as coarse meadow or tillage; but the strip was narrow—a man might throw a stone across it at some points—and on either side the heath and gorse and fern held their own on the dry sand. Such a place afforded no room for an English village of the true manorial kind; and I surmise that it lay all but uninhabited until perhaps the middle of the eighteenth century, by which time a few " squatters " from neighbouring parishes had probably settled here, to make what living they might beside the stream-bed. At no time, therefore, did the people form a group of genuinely agricultural rustics. Up to a period within living memory, they were an almost independent folk, leading a sort of "crofter," or (as I have preferred to call it) a "peasant" life; while to-day the majority of the men, no longer independent, go out to work as railway navvies, builders' labourers, drivers of vans and carts in the town; or are more casually employed at digging gravel, or road-mending, or harvesting and hay-making, or attending people's gardens, or laying sewers, or in fact at any job they can find. At a low estimate nine out of every ten of them get their living outside the parish boundaries; and this fact by itself would rob the place of its title to be thought a village, in the strict sense.

In appearance, too, it is abnormal. As you look down upon the valley from its high sides, hardly anywhere are there to be seen three cottages in a row, but all about the steep slopes the little mean dwelling-places are scattered in disorder. So it extends east and west for perhaps a mile and a half—a surprisingly populous hollow now, wanting in restfulness to the eyes and much disfigured by shabby detail, as it winds away into homelier and softer country at either end. The high-road out of the town, stretching away for Hindhead and the South Coast, comes slanting down athwart the valley, cutting it into "Upper" and "Lower" halves or ends; and just in the bottom, where there is a bridge over the stream, the appearances might deceive a stranger into thinking that he had come to the nucleus of an old village, since a dilapidated farmstead and a number of cottages line the sides of the road at that point. The appearances, however, are deceptive. I doubt if the cottages are more than a century old; and even if any of them have a greater antiquity, still it is not as the last relics of an earlier village that they are to be regarded. On the contrary, they indicate the beginnings of the present village. Before them, their place was unoccupied, and they do but commemorate the first of that series of changes by which the valley has been turned from a desolate wrinkle in the heaths into the anomalous suburb it has become to-day.

Of the period and manner of that first change I have already given a hint, attributing it indefinitely to a slow immigration of squatters somewhere in the eighteenth century. Neither the manner of it, however, nor the period is material here. Let it suffice that, a hundred years ago or so, the valley had become inhabited by people living in the " peasant " way presently to be described more fully. The subject of this book begins with the next change, which by and by overtook these same people, and dates from the enclosure of the common, no longer ago than 1861. The enclosure was effected in the usual fashion : a few adjacent landowners obtained the lion's share, while the cottagers came in for small allotments. These allotments, of little use to their owners, and in many cases soon sold for a few pounds apiece, became the sites of the first few cottages for a newer population, who slowly drifted in and settled down, as far as might be, to the habits and outlook of their predecessors. This second period continued until about 1900. And now, during the last ten years, a yet greater change has been going on. The valley has been " discovered " as a " residential centre." A water-company gave the signal for development. No sooner was a good water-supply available than speculating architects and builders began to buy up vacant plots of land, or even cottages—it mattered little which—and what never was strictly speaking a village is at last ceasing even to think itself one. The population of some five hundred twenty years ago has increased to over two thousand; the final shabby patches of the old heath are disappearing; on all hands glimpses of new building and raw new roads defy you to persuade yourself that you are in a country place. In fact, the place is a suburb of the town in the next valley, and the once quiet high-road is noisy with the motor-cars of the richer residents and all the town traffic that waits upon the less wealthy.

But although in the exactest sense the parish was never a village, its inhabitants, as lately as twenty years ago (when I came to live here) had after all a great many of the old English country characteristics. Dependent on the town for their living the most of them may have been by that time; yet they had derived their outlook and their habits from the earlier half-squatting, half-yeoman people; so that I found myself amongst neighbours rustic enough to justify me in speaking of them as villagers. I have come across their like elsewhere, and I am not deceived. They had the country touch. They were a survival of the England that is dying out now; and I grieve that I did not realize it sooner. As it was, some years had passed by, and the movement by which I find myself living to-day in a " residential centre " was already faintly stirring before I began to discern properly that the earlier circumstances would repay closer attention.

They were not all agreeable circumstances; some of them, indeed, were so much the reverse of agreeable that I hardly see now how I could ever have found them even tolerable. The want of proper sanitation, for instance; the ever-recurring scarcity of water; the plentiful signs of squalid and disordered living—how unpleasant they all must have been! On the other hand, some of the circumstances were so acceptable that, to recover them, I could at times almost be willing to go back and endure the others. It were worth something to renew the old lost sense of quiet; worth something to be on such genial terms with one's neighbours; worth very much to become acquainted again at first hand with the customs and modes of thought that prevailed in those days. Here at my door people were living, in many respects, by primitive codes which have now all but disappeared from England, and things must have been frequently happening such as, henceforth, will necessitate journeys into other countries if one would see them.

I remember yet how subtly the intimations of a primitive

mode of living used to reach me before I had learnt to appreciate their meaning. Unawares an impression of antiquity would come stealing over the senses, on a November evening, say, when the blue wood-smoke mounted from a cottage chimney and went drifting slowly down the valley in level layers; or on still summer afternoons, when there came up from the hollow the sounds of haymaking—the scythe shearing through the grass, the clatter of the whetstone, the occasional country voices. The dialect, and the odd ideas expressed in it, worked their elusive magic over and over again. To hear a man commend the weather, rolling out his " Nice moarnin' " with the fat Surrey " R," or to be wished " Good-day, sir," in the high twanging voice of some cottage-woman or other, was to be reminded in one's senses, without thinking about it at all, that one was amongst people not of the town, and hardly of one's own era. The queer things, too, which one happened to hear of, the simple ideas which seemed so much at home in the valley, though they would have been so much to be deprecated in the town, all contributed to produce the same old-world impression. Where the moon's changes were discussed so solemnly, and people numbered the " mistis in March " in expectation of corresponding " frostis in May "; where, if a pig fell sick, public opinion counselled killing it betimes, lest it should die and be considered unfit for food; where the most time-honoured saying was counted the best wit, so that you raised a friendly smile by murmuring " Good for young ducks " when it rained; where the names of famous sorts of potatoes— red-nosed kidneys, *magnum bonums*, and so on—were better known than the names of politicians or of newspapers; where spades and reap-hooks of well-proved quality were treasured as friends by their owners and coveted by other connoisseurs—it was impossible that one should not be frequently visited by the feeling of something very old-fashioned in the human life surrounding one.

More pointed in their suggestion of a rustic tradition were

the various customs and pursuits proper to given seasons. The customs, it is true, were preserved only by the children; but they had their acceptable effect. It might have been foolish and out-of-date, yet it was undeniably pleasant to know on May Day that the youngsters were making holiday from school, and to have them come to the door with their morning faces, bringing their buttercup garlands and droning out the appropriate folk ditty. At Christmastime, too, it was pleasant when they came singing carols after dark. This, indeed, they still do; but either I am harder to please or the performance has actually degenerated, for I can no longer discover in it the simple childish spirit that made it gratifying years ago.

Meanwhile, quite apart from such celebrations, the times and seasons observed by the people in following their work gave a flavour of folk manners which dignified the life of the parish, by associating it with the doings of the countryside for many generations. In August, though one did not see, one heard about, the gangs of men trudging off at night for the Sussex harvest. In September the days went very silently in the valley, because the cottages were shut up and people were all away at the hop-picking; and then, in the gathering dusk, one heard the buzz and rumour of manifold homecomings—tired children squalling, women talking and perhaps scolding, as the little chattering groups came near and passed out of earshot to their several cottages; while, down the hollows, hovering in the crisp night air, drifted a most appetizing smell of herrings being fried for a late meal. Earlier in the year there was hay-making in the valley itself. All the warm night was sometimes fragrant with the scent of cut grass; and about this season, too, the pungent odour of shallots lying out in the gardens to ripen off would come in soft whiffs across the hedges. Always, at all times, the people were glad to gossip about their gardens, bringing vividly into one's thoughts the homely importance of the month, nay, the very week, that was passing. Now, around Good Friday, the talk would be of potato-planting; and again, in proper order, one heard of peas and runner-beans, and so through the summer fruits and plants, to the ripening of plums and apples, and the lifting of potatoes and carrots and parsnips.

In all these ways the parish, if not a true village, seemed quite a country place twenty years ago, and its people were country people. Yet there was another side to the picture. The charm of it was a generalized one—I think an impersonal one; for with the thought of individual persons who might illustrate it there comes too often into my memory a touch of sordidness, if not in one connection then in another; so that I suspect myself, not for the first time, of sentimentality. Was the social atmosphere after all anything but a creation of my own dreams? Was the village life really idyllic?

Not for a moment can I pretend that it was. Patience and industry dignified it; a certain rough jollity, a large amount of good temper and natural kindness, kept it from being foul; but of the namby-pamby or soft-headed sentiment which many writers have persuaded us to attribute to old-English cottage life I think I have not in twenty years met with a single trace. In fact, there are no people so likely to make ridicule of that sort of thing as my labouring-class neighbours have always been. They do not, like the middle classes, enjoy it. It is a commodity for which they have no use, as may appear in the following pages.

To say this, however, is to say too little. I do not mean that the prevailing temper in the village was sordid, bitter, cruel, like that, say, of the Norman peasantry in De Maupassant's short stories. In by far the greater majority the people have usually seemed to me at the worst a little suspicious, a little callous, a little undemonstrative, and at the best generous and happy-go-lucky to a fault. Nevertheless, tales as repulsive as any that the French writer has told of his country-people could have been collected here by anyone with a taste for that sort of thing. Circumstantial narratives have reached me of savage, or, say, brutish, doings: of sons ill-treating their mothers, and husbands their wives! of fights, and cruelties, and sometimes— not often—of infamous vice. The likelihood of these tales, which there was no reason to doubt, was strengthened by what I saw and heard for myself. Drunkenness corrupted and disgraced the village life, so that good men went wrong and their families suffered miserably. I have helped more than one drunkard home at night, and seen a wretched woman or a frightened child come to the door to receive him. Even in the seclusion of my own garden I could not escape the evidences of mischief going on. For sounds echo up and down the valley as clearly as across the water of a lake; and sometimes a quiet evening would grow suddenly horrid with distracted noises of family quarrel in some distant cottage, when women shrilled and clamoured and men cursed, and all the dogs in the parish fell a-barking furiously. Even in bed one could not be secure. Once or twice some wild cry in the night—a woman's scream, a man's volley of oaths—has drawn me hurrying to my window in dread that outrage was afoot; and often the sounds of obscene singing from the road, where men were blundering homewards late from the public-houses in the town, have startled me out of my first sleep. Then, besides the distresses brought upon the people by their own folly, there were others thrust upon them by their economic condition. Of poverty, with its attendant sicknesses and neglects, there has never been any end to the tales, while the desolations due to accidents in the day's work, on the railway, or with horses, or upon scaffoldings of buildings, or in collapsing gravel-quarries, have become almost a commonplace. In short, there is no room for sentimentality about the village life. Could its annals be written they would make no idyll; they would be too much stained by tragedy and vice and misery.

Yet the knowledge of all this—and it was not possible to live here long without such knowledge—left the other impressions I have spoken of quite unimpaired. Disorders were the exception, after all. As a general rule the village character was genial, steadfast, self-respecting; one could not but recognize in it a great fund of strength, a great stability; nor could one help feeling that its main features—the limitations and the grimness, as well as the surprising virtues—were somehow closely related to that pleasant order of things suggested by the haymaking sounds, by the smell of the wood-smoke, by the children's May-day garlands. And, in fact, the relationship was essential. The temper and manners of the older people turned out to have been actually moulded by conditions of a true village kind, so that the same folk-quality that sounded in the little garland song reappeared more sternly in my neighbours' attitude towards their fate. Into this valley, it is true, much had never come that had flourished and been forgotten in English villages elsewhere. At no time had there been any of the more graceful folk arts here; at no time any comely social life, such as one reads of in Goldsmith's *Deserted Village* or Gray's *Elegy*; but, as I gradually learnt, the impoverished labouring people I talked to had been, in many cases, born in the more prosperous conditions of a self-supporting peasantry.

Bit by bit the truth come home to me, in the course of unconcerned gossip, when my informants had no idea of the significance of those stray scraps of information which they let fall. I was not alive to it myself for a long time. But when I had heard of the village cows, which used to be turned out to graze on the heaths, and had been told how fir-timber fit for cottage roof-joists could be cut on the common, as well as heath good enough for thatching and turf excellent for firing; and when to this was added the talk of bread-ovens at half the old cottages, and of little corn-crops in the gardens, and of brewing and wine-making and bee-keeping; I understood at last that my elderly neighbours had seen with their own eyes what I should never see—namely, the old rustic economy of the English peasantry. In that light all sorts of things showed a new meaning. I looked with rather changed sentiments, for example, upon the noisome pigstyes—for were they not a survival of a venerable thrift? I viewed the old tools—hoes and spades and scythes and fag-hooks—with quickened interest; and I speculated with more intelligence upon those aged people of the parish whose curious habits were described to me with so much respect. But of all the details that now gained significance, most to be noted were the hints of the comparative prosperity of that earlier time. For now some old woman, half starving on her parish pay, would indicate this or that little cottage, and remark that her grandfather had built it for her mother to go into when she married. Or now, a decrepit man would explain that in such and such a puzzling nook in the hillside had once stood his father's cow-stall. Here, at the edge of the arable strip, a building divided into two poor cottages proved to have been originally somebody's little hop-kiln; there, on a warm slope given over to the pleasure-garden of some "resident" like myself, a former villager used to grow enough wheat to keep him in flour half the winter; and there again, down a narrow by-way gone ruinous from long neglect, Master So-and-so, whose children to-day go in fear of the workhouse, was wont to drive his little waggon and pair of horses.

Particulars like these, pointing to a lost state of well-being, accounted very well for the attraction which, in spite of individual faults, I had felt towards the village folk in general. The people stood for something more than merely themselves. In their odd ways and talk and character I was affected, albeit unawares, by a robust tradition of the English countryside, surviving here when the circumstances which would have explained it had already largely disappeared. After too many years of undiscernment that truth was apparent to me. And even so, it was but a gradual enlightenment; even now it is unlikely that I appreciate the facts in their deepest significance. For the "robust" tradition, as I have just called it, was something more than simply robust. It was older, by far, than this anomalous village. Imported into the valley—if my surmise is correct—by squatters two centuries ago, it was already old even then; it already had centuries of experience behind it; and though it very likely had lost much in that removal, still it was a genuine off-shoot of the home-made or " folk " civilization of the South of England. No wonder that its survivals had struck me as venerable and pleasant, when there was so much vigorous English life behind them, derived perhaps from so many fair English counties.

The perception came to me only just in time, for to-day the opportunities of further observation occur but rarely. The old life is being swiftly obliterated. The valley is passing out of the hands of its former inhabitants. They are being crowded into corners, and are becoming as aliens in their own home; they are receding before newcomers with new ideas, and, greatest change of all, they are yielding to the dominion of new ideas themselves. At present, therefore, the cottagers are a most heterogeneous population, presenting all sorts of baffling problems to those who have to deal with them, as the school-master and the sanitary officer and others find. In no two families—hardly in two members of the same family—do the old traditions survive in equal degree. A lath-and-plaster partition may separate people who are half a century asunder in civilization, and on the same bench at school may be found side by side two children who come from homes, the one worthy of King George III.'s time, the other not unworthy of King George V.'s. But the changes which will remove the greatest of these discrepancies are proceeding very fast; in another ten years' time there will be not much left of the traditional life whose crumbling away I have been witnessing during the twenty years that are gone.

Some grounds of hope—great hope, too—which begin at last to appear, and are treated of in the final chapter of this book, save the tale of Change in the Village from being quite a tragedy, yet still it is a melancholy tale. I have dealt with it in the two sections called respectively " The Altered Circumstances" and "The Resulting Needs." The earlier chapters, which immediately follow this one under the heading "The Present Time," are merely descriptive of the people and their conditions as I know them now, and aim at nothing more than to pave the way for a clearer understanding of the main subject.

II

THE PRESENT TIME

II

SELF-RELIANCE

THERE is a chapter in Dickens's *Hard Times* which tells how it was discovered that somebody had fallen down a disused mine-shaft, and how the rescue was valiantly effected by a few men who had to be awakened for that end from their drunken Sunday afternoon sleep. Sobered by the dangers they foresaw, these men ran to the pit-mouth, pushed straight to the centre of the crowd there, and fell to work quietly with their ropes and winches. As you read, you seem to see them, spitting on their great hands while they knot the ropes, listening attentively to the doctor as to an equal, and speaking in undertones to one another, but regardless of the remarks of the bystanders. The best man amongst them, says Dickens—and you know it to be true : Dickens could have told you the men's names and life-history had he chosen—the best man amongst them was the greatest drunkard of the lot; and when his heroic work was done, nobody seems to have taken any further notice of him.

These were Northcountrymen; but there was a quality about them of which I have often been reminded, in watching or hearing tell of the men in this Surrey village. It is the thing that most impresses all who come into any sympathetic contact with my neighbours : their readiness to make a start at the dangerous or disagreeable task when others would be still talking, and their apparent expectation that they will succeed. In this spirit they occasionally do things quite as well worthy of mention as the incident described by Dickens. I remember looking on myself at just such another piece of work, in the town a mile away from here, one winter day. The sluggish " river," as we call it, which flows amongst meadows on the south of the town, is usually fordable beside one of the bridges, and men with horses and carts as often as not drive through the ford, instead of going over the bridge. But on the day I am recalling floods had so swollen the stream that a horse and cart were swept down under the narrow bridge, and had got jammed there, the driver having escaped over the iron railings of the bridge as the cart went under. I don't know what became of him then—he was but a lad, I was told. When I came on the scene, a number of people were on the bridge, while many more were down on the river banks, whence they could see the horse and cart under the arch. A few were bawling out unheeded advice as to what should be done; in fact, a heated altercation had arisen between the two loudest—a chimney-sweep and a medical man—whose theories disagreed; but it was plain to everybody that it would be a risky thing to venture under the bridge into that swirling stream. For ten minutes or more, while the horse remained invisible to us on the bridge, and likely to drown, the dispute snapped angrily from bank to bank, punctuated occasionally by excited cries, such as " He's gettin' lower!" " He's sinkin' down!" Then, unobserved, a bricklayer's labourer came running with a rope, which he hurriedly made into a noose and tightened under his armpits. None of the shouters, by the way, had suggested such a plan. The man was helped over the railings and swiftly lowered—Heaven knows who took a hand at that—and so he disappeared for five minutes. Then a shout: the horse came into view, staggering downstream with harness cut, and scrambled up into the meadow; and the man, drenched and deadly white, and too benumbed to help himself, was hauled up on to the bridge, and carried to the nearest inn. I never heard his name—people of his sort, as Dickens knew, are generally anonymous—but he was one of the labourers of the locality, and only last winter I saw him shivering at the street corners amongst other out-o'-works.

Behaviour like this is so characteristic of labouring men that we others expect it of them as if it were especially their duty. Again and again I have noticed it. If a horse falls in the street, ten chances to one it is some obscure labouring fellow who gets him up again. Whether there is danger or no, in emergencies which demand readiness and disregard of comfort, the common unskilled labourer is always to the fore. One summer night I had strolled out to the top of the road here which slants down, over-arched by tall trees, past the Vicarage. At some distance down, where there should have been such a depth of darkness under the trees, I was surprised to see a little core of light, where five or six people stood around a bright lamp, which one of them was holding. The scene looked so theatrical, glowing under the trees with the summer night all round it, that, of course, I had to go down the hill and investigate it. The group I joined was, it turned out, watching a bicyclist who lay unconscious in somebody's arms, while a doctor fingered at a streaming wound in the man's forehead, and washed it, and finally stitched it up. The bicycle—its front wheel buckled by collision with the Vicarage gatepost—stood against the gate, and two or three cushions lay in the hedge; for the Vicar had come out to the man's assistance, and had sent for the doctor, and it was the Vicar himself, old and grey, but steady, who now held his library lamp for the doctor's use. The rest of us stood looking on, one of us at least feeling rather sick at the sight, and all of us as useless as the night-moths which came out from the trees and fluttered round the lamp. At last, when all was done, and the injured man could be moved, there rose up a hitherto unnoticed fellow who had been supporting him, and I recognized one of our village labourers. He looked faint, and tottered to a chair which the Vicar had ready, and gulped at some brandy, for he, too, had been overcome by the sight of the surgery. But it was to him that the task of sitting in the dusty road and being smeared with blood had fallen.

And this quiet acceptance of the situation, recognizing that he if anyone must suffer, and take the hard place which soils the clothes and shocks the feelings, gives the clue to the average labourer's temper. It is really very curious to think of. Rarely can a labourer afford the luxury of a " change." Wet through though his clothes may be, or blood-stained, or smothered with mud or dust, he must wear them until he goes to bed, and must put them on again as he finds them in the morning; but this does not excuse him in our eyes from taking the disagreeable place. Still less does it excuse him in his own eyes. If you offer to help, men of this kind will probably dissuade you. " It'll make yer clothes all dirty," they say; " you'll get in such a mess." So they assume the burden, sometimes surly and swearing, oftener with a good-tempered jest.

To anything with a touch of humour in it they will leap forward like schoolboys. I am reminded of a funny incident one frosty morning, when patches of the highway were slippery as glass. Preceding me along the road was a horse and cart, driven by a boy who stood upright in the cart, and seemed not to notice how the horse's hoofs were skidding; and some distance ahead three railway navvies were approaching, just off their night's work, and carrying their picks and shovels. I had left the cart behind, and was near these three, when suddenly they burst into a laugh, exclaiming to one another, " Look at that old 'oss!" I turned. There sat the horse on his tail between the shafts, pawing with his feet at the road, but unable to get a grip at its slippery surface. It was impossible not to smile; he had such an absurd look. The navvies, however, did more than smile. They broke into a run; they saw immediately what to do. In thirty seconds they were shovelling earth out from the hedgerow under the horse's feet, and in two minutes more he had scrambled up, unhurt.

In such behaviour, I say, we have a clue to the labouring-man's temper. The courage, the carelessness of discomfort, the swiftness to see what should be done, and to do it, are not inspired by any tradition of chivalry, any consciously elaborated cult. It is habitual with these men to be ready, and those fine actions which win our admiration are but chance disclosures in public of a self-reliance constantly practised by the people amongst themselves—by the women quite as much as by the men—under stress of necessity, one would say at first sight. Take another example of the same willing efficiency applied in rather a different way. In a cottage near to where I am writing a young labourer died last summer—a young unmarried man, whose mother was living with him, and had long depended on his support. Eighteen months earlier he had been disabled for a week or two by the kick of a horse, and a heart-disease of long standing was so aggravated by the accident that he was never again able to do much work. There came months of unemployment, and as a consequence he was in extreme poverty when he died. His mother was already reduced to parish relief; it was only by the help of his two sisters—young women out at service, who managed to pay for a coffin for him—that a pauper's funeral was avoided. A labourer's wife, the mother of four or five young children, took upon herself the duty of washing and laying out the corpse, but there remained still the funeral to be managed. An undertaker to conduct it could not be engaged; there was no money to pay him. Then, however, neighbours took the matter up, not as an unwonted thing, I may say—it is usual with them to help bury a " mate " —only, as a rule, there is the undertaker too. In this case they did without him—six poor men losing half a day's work, and giving their services. The coffin was too big to be carried down the crooked staircase; too big also to be got out of the bedroom window until the window-sashes had been taken out. But these men managed it all, borrowing tools and a couple of ladders and some ropes; and then, in the black clothes which they kept for such occasions, they carried the coffin to the churchyard. That same evening two of them went to work at cleaning out a cess-pit, two others spent the evening in their gardens, another had cows to milk, and the sixth, being out of work and restless, had no occupation to go home to so far as I know.

Of course this, too, was a piece of voluntary service, resembling in that respect those more striking examples of self-reliance which are brought out by sudden emergencies. But it points, more directly than they do, to the sphere in which that virtue is practised until it becomes a habit. For if you follow the clue on, it leads very quickly to the scene where self-reliance is so to speak at home, where it seems the natural product of the people's circumstances—the scene, namely, of their daily work. For there, not only in the employment by which the men earn their wages, but in the household and garden work of the women as well as the men, there is nothing to support them save their own readiness, their own personal force.

It sounds a truism, but it is worth attention. Unlike the rest of us, labouring people are unable to shirk any of life's discomforts by " getting a man " or " a woman," as we say, to do the disagreeable or risky jobs which continually need to be done. If a cottager in this village wants his chimney swept, or his pigstye cleaned out, or his firewood chopped, the only " man " he can get to do it for him is himself. Similarly with his wife. She may not call in " a woman " to scrub her floor, or to wash and mend, or to skin a rabbit for dinner, or to make up the fire for cooking it. It is necessary for her to be ready to turn from one task to another without squeamishness, and without pausing to think how she shall do it. In short, she and her husband alike must practise, in their daily doings, a sort of intrepidity which grows customary with them; and this habit is the parent of much of that fine conduct which they exhibit so carelessly in moments of emergency.

Until this fact is appreciated there is no such thing as understanding the people's disposition. It is the principal gateway that lets you in to their character. Nevertheless the subject needs no further illustration here. Anyone personally acquainted with the villagers knows how their life is one continuous act of unconscious self-reliance, and those who have not seen it for themselves will surely discover plentiful evidences of it in the following pages, if they read between the lines.

But I must digress to remark upon one aspect of the matter. In view of the subject of this book—namely, the transition from an old social order to present times—it should be considered whether the handiness of the villagers is after all quite so natural a thing as is commonly supposed. For a long time I took it for granted. The people's accomplishments were rough, I admit, and not knowing how much " knack " or experience was involved in the dozens of odd jobs that they did, I assumed that they did them by the light of Nature. Yet if we reflect how little we learn from Nature, and how helpless people grow after two or three generations of life in slums, or in libraries and drawing-rooms, it would seem probable that there is more on the surface in the labourer's versatility of usefulness. After all, who would know by the light of Nature how to go about sweeping a chimney, as they used to do it here, with rope and furze-bush dragged down? or how to scour out a water-tank effectively? or where to begin upon cleaning a pigstye? Easy though it looks, the closer you get down to this kind of work as the cottager does it the more surprisedly do you discover that he recognizes right and wrong methods of doing it; and my own belief is that the necessity which compels the people to be their own servants would not make them so adaptable as they are, were there not, at the back of them, a time-honoured tradition teaching them how to go on.

Returning from this digression, and speaking, too, rather of a period from ten to twenty years ago than of the present time, it would be foolish to pretend that the people's good qualities were unattended by defects. The men had a very rough exterior, so rough that I have known them to inspire timidity in the respectable who met them on the road, and especially at night, when, truth to tell, those of them who were out were not always too sober. After you got to know them, so as to understand the shut of their mouths and the look of their eyes —usually very steadfast and quiet—you knew that there was rarely any harm in them; but I admit that their aspect was unpromising enough at first sight. A stranger might have been forgiven for thinking them coarse, ignorant, stupid, beery, unclean. And yet there was excuse for much of it, while much more of it was sheer ill-fortune, and needed no excuse. Though many of the men were physically powerful, few of them could boast of any physical comeliness. Their strength had been bought dear, at the cost of heavy labour begun too early in life, so that before middle age they were bent in the back, or gone wrong at the knees, and their walk (some of them walked miles every day to their work) was a long shambling stride, fast enough, but badly wanting in suggestiveness of personal pride. Seeing them casually in their heavy and uncleanly clothes, no one would have dreamed of the great qualities in them—the kindliness and courage and humour, the readiness to help, the self-control, the patience. It was all there, but they took no pains to look the part; they did not show off.

In fact, their tendency was rather in the contrary direction. They cared too little what was thought of them to be at the pains of shocking one's delicacy intentionally; but they were by no means displeased to be thought " rough." It made them laugh; it was a tribute to their stout-heartedness. Nor was there anything necessarily braggart in this attitude of theirs. As they realized that work would not be readily offered to a man who might quail before its unpleasantness, so it was a matter of bread-and-cheese to them to cultivate " roughness."

I need not, indeed, be writing in the past tense here. It is still bad policy for a workman to be nice in his feelings, and several times I have had men excuse themselves for a weakness which they knew me to share, but which they seemed to think needed apology when they, too, exhibited it. Only a few weeks ago a neighbour's cat, affected with mange, was haunting my garden, and had become a nuisance. Upon my asking the owner—a labourer who had worked up to be something of a bricklayer—to get rid of it, he said he would get a certain old-fashioned neighbour to kill it, and then he plunged into sheepish explanations why he would rather not do the deed himself. " Anybody else's cat," he urged, " he wouldn't mind so much," but he had a touch of softness towards his own. It was plain that in reality he was a man of tender feelings, yet it was no less plain that he was unwilling to be thought too tender. The curious thing was that neither of us considered for a moment the possibility of any reluctance staying the hand of the older neighbour. Him we both knew fairly well as a man of that earlier period with which I am concerned just now. At that period the village in general had a lofty contempt for the " meek-hearted " man capable of flinching. An employer might have qualms, though the men thought no better of him for that possession, but amongst themselves flinching was not much other than a vice. In fact, they dared not be delicate. Hence through all their demeanour they displayed a hardness which in some cases went far below the surface, and approached real brutality.

Leaving out the brutality, the women were not very different from the men. It might have been supposed that their domestic work—the cooking and cleaning and sewing from which middle-class women seem often to derive so comely a manner—would have done something to soften these cottage women. But it rarely worked out so. The women shared the men's carelessness and roughness. That tenderness which an emergency discovered in them was hidden in everyday life under

manners indicative of an unfeigned contempt for what was
gentle, what was soft.

And this, too, was reasonable. In theory, perhaps, the
women should have been refined by their housekeeping work;
in practice that work necessitated their being very tough. Cook,
scullery-maid, bed-maker, charwoman, laundress, children's
nurse—it fell to every mother of a family to play all the parts in
turn every day, and if that were all, there was opportunity
enough for her to excel. But the conveniences which made
such work tolerable in other households were not to be found
in the cottage. Everything had to be done practically in one
room—which was sometimes a sleeping-room too, or say in one
room and a wash-house. The preparation and serving of meals,
the airing of clothes and the ironing of them, the washing of
the children, the mending and making—how could a woman
do any of it with comfort in the cramped apartment, into which,
moreover, a tired and dirty man came home in the evening to
eat and wash and rest, or if not to rest, then to potter in and
out from garden or pigstye, "treading in dirt" as he came?
Then, too, many cottages had not so much as a sink where
work with water could be done; many had no water save in
wet weather; there was not one cottage in which it could be
drawn from a tap, but it all had to be fetched from well or
tank. And in the husband's absence at work, it was the
woman's duty—one more added to so many others—to bring
water indoors. In times of drought water had often to be
carried long distances in pails, and it may be imagined how the
housework would go in such circumstances. For my part I
have never wondered at roughness or squalor in the village
since that parching summer when I learnt that in one cottage
at least the people were saving up the cooking water of one day
to be used over again on the day following. Where such things
can happen the domestic arts are simplified to nothing, and it
would be madness in women to cultivate refinement or niceness.

And my neighbours appeared not to wish to cultivate them.

It may be added that many of the women—the numbers are diminishing rapidly—were field-workers who had never been brought up to much domesticity. Far beyond the valley they had to go to earn money at hop-tying, haymaking, harvesting, potato-picking, swede-trimming, and at such work they came immediately, just as the men did, under conditions which made it a vice to flinch. As a rule they would leave work in the afternoon in time to get home and cook a meal in readiness for their husbands later, and at that hour one saw them on the roads trudging along, under the burden of coats, dinner-baskets, tools, and so on, very dishevelled—for at field-work there is no such thing as care for the toilet—but often chatting not un-happily.

On the roads, too, women were, and still are, frequently noticeable, bringing home on their backs faggots of dead wood, or sacks of fir-cones, picked up in the fir-woods a mile away or more. Prodigious and unwieldy loads these were. I have often met women bent nearly double under them, toiling painfully along, with hats or bonnets pushed awry and skirts draggling. Occasionally tiny urchins, too small to be left at home alone, would be clinging to their mothers' frocks.

In the scanty leisure that the women might enjoy—say now and then of an afternoon—there were not many circumstances to counteract the hardness contracted at their work. These off times were opportunities for social intercourse between them. They did not leave home, however, and go out " paying calls." Unless on Sunday evenings visiting one another's cottages was not desirable. But there were other resources. I have men-tioned how sounds will travel across the valley, and I have known women come to their cottage doors high up on this side to carry on a shouting conversation with neighbours opposite, four hundred yards away. You see, they were under no con-straint of propriety in its accepted forms, nor did they care greatly who heard what they had to say. I have sometimes wished that they did care. But, of course, the more comfort-

able way of intercourse was to talk across the quickset hedge
between two gardens. Sometimes one would hear—all an
afternoon it seemed—the long drone of one of these confabulations going on in unbroken flow, with little variation of
cadence, save for a moaning rise and fall, like the wind through
a keyhole. I have a suspicion that the shortcomings of neighbours often made the staple of such conversations, but that is
only a surmise. I remember the strange conclusion of one of
them which reached my ears. For, as the women reluctantly
parted, they raised their voices, and one said piously, " Wal,
they'll git paid for 't, one o' these days. Gawd A'mighty's
above the Devil "; to which the other, with loud conviction :
" Yes, and always will be, thank Gawd ! " This ended the
talk. But the last speaker, turning round, saw her two-year-old
daughter asprawl in the garden, and with sudden change from
satisfied drawl to shrill exasperation, " Git up out of all that
muck, you dirty little devil," she said. For she was a cleanly
woman, proud of her children, and disliking to see them un-
tidy.

III

MAN AND WIFE

FOR general social intercourse the labouring people do not meet
at one another's cottages, going out by invitation, or dropping
in to tea in the casual way of friendship; they have to be content
with " passing the time of day " when they come together by
chance. Thus two families may mingle happily as they stroll
homewards after the Saturday night's shopping in the town, or
on a fine Sunday evening they may make up little parties to go
and inspect one another's gardens.

Until recently—so recently that the slight change may be ignored at least for the present—the prevailing note of this so restricted intercourse was a sort of *bonhomie,* or good temper and good sense. With this for a guide, the people had no need of the etiquette called " good manners," but were at liberty to behave as they liked, and talk as they liked, within the bounds of neighbourliness and civility. This has always been one of the most conspicuous things about the people—this independence of conventions. In few other grades of society could men and women dare to be so outspoken together, so much at ease, as these villagers still often are. Their talk grows Chaucerian at times. Merrily, or seriously, as the case may be, subjects are spoken of which are never alluded to between men and women who respect our ordinary conventions.

Let it be admitted—if anybody wishes to feel superior—that the women must be wanting in "delicacy" to countenance such things. There are other aspects of the matter which are better worth considering. Approaching it, for instance, from an opposite point of view, one perceives that the average country labourer can talk with less restraint because he has really less to conceal than many men who look down upon him. He may use coarse words, but his thoughts are wont to be cleanly, so that there is no suspicion of foulness behind his conversation, rank though it sound. A woman consequently may hear what he says, and not be offended by suggestion of something left unsaid. On these terms the jolly tale is a jolly tale, and ends at that. It does not linger to corrupt the mind with an unsavoury after-flavour.

But more than this is indicated by the want of conventional manners in the village. The main fact is that the two sexes, each engaged daily upon essential duties, stand on a surprising equality the one to the other. And where the men are so well aware of the women's experienced outlook, and the women so well aware of the men's, the affectation of ignorance might almost be construed as a form of immodesty, or at any rate as an imprudence. It would, indeed, be too absurd to pretend that these wives and mothers, who have to face every trial of life and death for themselves, do not know the things which obviously they cannot help knowing; too absurd to treat them as though they were all innocence, and timidity, and daintiness. No labouring man would esteem a woman for delicacy of that kind, and the women certainly would not like to be esteemed for it. Hence the sexes habitually meet on almost level terms. And the absence of convention extends to a neglect—nay, to a dislike—of ordinary graceful courtesies between them. So far as I have seen they observe no ceremonial. The men are considerate to spare women the more exhausting or arduous kinds of work; but they will let a woman open the door for herself, and will be careless when they are together who stands or who sits, or which of them walks on the inside of the path, or goes first into a gateway. And the women look for nothing different. They expect to be treated as equals. If a cottage woman found that a cottage man was raising his hat to her, she would be aflame with indignation, and would let him know very plainly indeed that she was not that sort of fine lady.

In general, the relations between the sexes are too matter-of-fact to permit of any refinement of feeling about them, and it is not surprising that illegitimacy has been very common in the village. But once a man and a woman are married, they settle down into a sober pair of comrades, and instead of the looseness which might be looked for there is on the whole a remarkable fidelity between the married couples. I have no distinct memory of having heard during twenty years of any certain case of intrigue or conjugal misbehaviour amongst the cottage folk. The people seem to leave that sort of thing to the employing classes. It scandalizes them to hear of it. They despise it. Oddly enough, this may be partly due to the want of a feminine ideal, such as is developed by help of our middle-class arts and recognized in our conventions. True, the business of making both ends meet provides the labourer and his wife with enough to think about, especially when the children begin to come. Then, too, they have no luxuries to pamper their flesh, no lazy hours in which to grow wanton. The severity of the man's daily labour keeps him quiet; the woman, drudge that she is, soon loses the surface charm that would excite admirers. But when all this is said, it remains probable that a lowliness in their ideal preserves the villagers from temptation. They do not put woman on a pedestal to be worshipped; they are unacquainted with the finer, more sensitive, more high-strung possibilities of her nature. People who have been affected by long traditions of chivalry, or by the rich influences of art, are in another case; but here amongst the labouring folk a woman is not seen through the medium of any cherished theories; she is merely an individual woman, a man's comrade and helper, and the mother of his family. It is a fine thing, though, about the unions effected on these unromantic terms, that they usually last long, the man and wife growing more affectionate, more tender, more trustful, as they advance in years.

Of course, the marriages are not invariably comfortable or even tolerable. One hears sometimes of men callously disappearing—deserting their wives for a period, and going off, as if for peace, to distant parts wherever there is work to be picked up. One man, I remember, was reported to have said, when he ultimately reappeared, that he had gone away because " he thought it would do his wife good." Another, who had openly quarrelled with his wife and departed, was discovered months afterwards working in a Sussex harvest-field. He came back by-and-by, and now for years the couple have been living together, not without occasional brawls, it's true, but in the main good comrades, certainly helpful to one another, and very fond of their two or three children. A bad case was that of a bullying railway navvy, who, having knocked his wife about and upset his old father, went off ostensibly to work. In reality he made his way by train to a town some ten miles distant, and from there, in a drunken frolic, sent a telegram home to his wife announcing that he was dead. He had given no particulars: a long search for him followed, and he was found some days later in a public-house of that town vaingloriously drinking. I remember that Bettesworth, who told me this tale, was full of indignation. " Shouldn't you think he could be punished for that?" he asked. " There, if I had my way he should have twelve months reg'lar *hard labour,* and see if that wouldn't dummer a little sense into 'n." There was no suggestion, however, of " a woman in the case," to explain this man's ill-treatment of his wife; it appears to have been simply a piece of freakish brutality.

When disagreements occur, it is likely that the men are oftener to blame than their wives. Too often I have seen some woman or other of the village getting her drunken and abusive husband home, and never once have I seen it the other way about. Nevertheless, in some luckless households the faults are on the woman's side, and it is the man who has the heartache. I knew one man—a most steady and industrious fellow, in constant work which kept him from home all day—whose wife became a sort of parasite on him in the interest of her own thriftless relatives. In his absence her brothers and sisters were at his table eating at his expense; food and coals bought with his earnings found their way to her mother's cottage; in short, he had " married the family," as they say. He knew it, too. In its trumpery way the affair was an open scandal, and the neighbours dearly wished to see him put a stop to it. Yet, though he would have had public opinion to support him in taking strong measures, his own good nature deterred him from doing so. Probably, too, his own course was the happier one. Thrive he never could, and gloomy enough and dispirited enough he used to look at times; yet to see him with his children on Sundays—two or three squalid, laughing urchins— was to see a very acceptable sight.

Returning to the main point, if anyone has a taste for ugly behaviour, and thinks nothing " real " but what is uncomfort able too, he may find plenty of subjects for study in the married life of this parish; but he will be ridiculously mistaken if he supposes the ugliness to be normal. A kind of dogged comradeship—I can find no better word for it—is what commonly unites the labouring man and his wife; they are partners and equals running their impecunious affairs by mutual help. I was lately able to observe a man and woman after a removal settling down into their new quarters. It was the most ordinary, matter-of-fact affair in the world. The man, uncouth and strong, like a big dog or an amiable big boy, moved about willingly under his wife's direction, doing the various jobs that required strength. One evening, in rain, his wife stood watching while he chopped away the wet summer grass that had grown tall under the garden hedge; then she pointed out four or five spots against the hedge, where he proceeded to put in wooden posts. Early the next morning there was a clothes-line between the posts, and the household washing was hanging from it. Nothing could have been more commonplace than the whole incident, but the commonness was the beauty of it. And it was done somehow in a way that warmed one to a feeling of great liking for those two people.

Very often it seems to be the woman who supplies the brains, and does the scheming, for the partnership. When old Bettesworth was on his last legs, as many as half a dozen different men applied to me for his job, of whom one, I very well remember, apologized for troubling me, but said his "missus" told him to come. Poor chap! it was his idea of courtesy to offer an apology, and it was the Old Adam in him that laid the blame on his wife, for really he desired very much to escape from his arduous night-work on the railway. At the same time there is not the least doubt that what he said was true; that he and his wife had talked the matter over, and that, when he proved timid of interviewing me, she forced him to come. Again, two or three winters ago, a man despairing of work in England, got in touch with some agency to assist him in emigrating to Canada. It was his wife then who went round the parish trying to raise the few extra pounds that he was to contribute. That was a case to fill comfortable people with uncomfortable shame. The woman, not more than five-and-twenty, would have been strikingly handsome if she had ever in her life had a fair chance; but as it was she looked half-starved, and she had a cough which made it doubtful if she would ever live to follow her husband to Canada. Still, she was playing her part as the man's comrade. As soon as he could save enough money he was to send for her and her baby, she said; in the meantime she would have to earn her own living by going out to day-work.

During the South African War there was many a woman in the village keeping things together at home while the men were at the front. They had to work and earn money just as they do when their men are beaten down at home. There was one woman who received from her husband a copy of verses composed by him and his companions during their occupation of a block-house on the veldt. Very proud of him, she took the verses to a printer, had them printed—just one single copy—and then had the printed copy framed to hang on the bedroom wall in her cottage. Her husband showed it to me there one day, mightily pleased with it and her.

Probably the people behind the counters at the provision shops in the town could tell many interesting things about the relations between married people of this class, for it is quite the common thing in the villages for a man and wife to lock up their cottage on a Saturday evening, and go off with the children to do the week's shopping together. On a nice night the town becomes thronged with them, and so do the shops, outside which, now and then, a passer-by may notice little consultations going on, and husband or wife—sometimes one, sometimes the other—handing over precious money to the other to be spent. And if it is rather painful to see the faces grow so strained and anxious over such trifling sums, on the other hand the signs of mutual confidence and support are comforting. Besides, anxiety is not the commonest note. The majority of the people make a little weekly festivity of this Saturday night's outing; they meet their friends in the street, have a chat, wind up with a visit to the public-house, and so homewards at any time between seven and ten o'clock, trooping up the hill happily enough as a rule. Now and then one comes across solitary couples making one another miserable. Thus one night I heard a woman's voice in the dark, very tired and faint, say, "It's a long hill!" to which the surly tones of a man replied: "'Ten't no longer than 'twas, is it?" Brutishness like this, however, is quite the exception.

As a sample of what is normal, take the following scraps of talk overheard one summer night some years ago. The people were late that night, and indeed, it was pleasant to be out. Not as yet were there any of those street lamps along the road which now make all nights alike dingy; but one felt as if walking into the unspoiled country. For though it was after ten, and the sky overcast, still one could see very clearly the glimmering road and the hedgerows in the soft midsummer twilight. Enjoying this tranquillity, I passed by a man and a woman with two children, and heard the man say invitingly: "Shall I carry the basket?" The wife answered: "'E en't 'eavy, Bill, thanks. . . . Only I got this 'ere little Rosy to git along."

Her voice sounded gentle and cheerful, and I tried to hear more, checking my pace. But the children were walking too slowly. I was getting out of earshot, missing the drift of the peaceful-sounding chatter, when presently the woman, as if turning to the other child, said more loudly: "Come along, Sonny!" The man added: "Hullo, old man! Come along! You'll be left behind!"

The children began prattling; their father and mother laughed; but I was leaving them farther and farther behind. Then, however, some other homeward-goer overtook the little family. For the talk grew suddenly louder, the woman beginning cheerily: "Hullo, Mr. Weatherall! 'Ow's your poor wife? . . . I didn't see as 'twas you, 'till this here little Rosy said . . ."

What Rosy had said I failed to catch. I missed also what followed, leading up to the woman's endearing remark: "This 'ere little Rosy, she's a reg'lar gal for cherries!" The neighbour seemed to say something; then the husband; then the neighbour again. And at that there came a burst of laughter, loudest from the woman, and Mr. Weatherall asked: "Didn't you never hear that afore?"

The woman, laughing still, was emphatic: "No; I'll take my oath as I never knowed that."

"Well, you knows it now, don't ye?"

"I ain't sure yet. I ain't had time to consider."

After that the subject changed. I heard the woman say: "I've had six gals an' only one boy—one out o' seven. Alice is out courtin'"; and then they seemed to get on to the question of ways and means. The last words that reached me were "Fivepence . . . tuppence-ha'penny;" but still, when I could no longer catch any details at all, the voices continued to sound pleasantly good-tempered.

IV

MANIFOLD TROUBLES

BESIDES the unrelieved hardness of daily life—the need, which never lifts from them, of making shift and doing all things for themselves—there has always been another influence at work upon my neighbours, leaving its indelible mark on them. Almost from infancy onwards, in a most personal and intimate way, they are familiar with harrowing experiences of calamity such as people who employ them are largely able to escape. The little children are not exempt. There being no nursemaids to take care of the children while fathers and mothers are busy, the tiniest are often entrusted to the perilous charge of others not quite so tiny, and occasionally they come to grief. Then too often the older children, who are themselves more secure for a few years, are eyewitnesses of occurrences such as more fortunate boys and girls are hardly allowed even to hear of. Nor is it only with the gory or horrible disaster that the people thus become too early acquainted. The nauseating details of sickness are better known and more openly discussed in the cottage than in comfortable middle-class homes. For it is all such a crowded business—that of living in these cramped dwellings. Besides, the injured and the sick, absorbed in the interest of their ailments, are amiably willing to give others an opportunity of sharing it. The disorder or the disablement is thus almost a family possession. An elderly man, who had offered to show me a terrible ulcer on his leg, smiled at my squeamishness, as if he pitied me, when I declined the privilege. "Why, the little un," he said, pointing to a four-year-old girl on the floor, " the little un rolls the bandage for me every evening, because I dresses'n here before the fire." That is the way in the labourer's cottage. Even where privacy is attempted for the sufferer's sake there is no refuge for the family from the evidence of suffering. The young people in one room may hardly avoid knowing and hearing where a man is dying, or a woman giving birth to a child, just the other side of a latched deal door.

In this connection it should be remembered how much more than their share of the afflictions of the community falls to the labouring people. The men's work naturally takes them where accidents happen, where disease is contracted. And then, from ignorance or the want of conveniences, from the need to continue wage-earning as long as endurance will hold out, and

also from the sheer carelessness which is a part of their necessary habit, both the men and the women not seldom allow
themselves to fall into sickness which a little self-indulgence, if
only they dared yield to it, would enable them to avoid. I
should not know how to begin counting the numbers I have
personally known enfeebled for life in this way. Things are
better now than they were twenty years ago; there are many
more opportunities than there used to be of obtaining rest or
nursing, but still the evil is widespread. Without going out of
my way at all, during the last fortnight I have heard of—have
almost stumbled across—three cases of the sort. The first was
that of a woman who had been taking in washing during her
husband's long illness. Meeting the man, who was beginning
to creep about again, I happened to ask how his wife was; and
he said that she was just able to keep going, but hardly knew
how to stand because of varicose veins in both legs. The
second case, too, was a woman's. She met me on the road, and
on the off chance asked if I could give her a letter of admission
to the County Hospital, and so save her the pain of going down
to the Vicarage to beg for a letter there. What was the matter?
"I give birth to twins five months ago," she said, "and since
then dropsy have set in. I gets heavier every day. The doctor
wants me to go to the hospital, and I was goin' to the Vicar to
ask for a letter, but I dreads comin' back up that hill." As it
was she had already walked half a mile. In the third case a
man's indifference to his own suffering was to blame for the
plight in which he found himself. Driving a van, he had
barked his shin against the iron step on the front of the van.
Just as the skin had begun to heal over he knocked it again,
severely, in exactly the same way, and he described to me the
immense size of the aggravated wound. But, as he said, he
had supposed it would get well, and, beyond tying his leg up
with a rag, he took no further trouble about it, until it grew so
bad that he was obliged to see a doctor. His account of the
interview went in this way : " ' How long since you done this?'

the doctor says. ' A month,' I says. ' Then you must be a damn fool not to 'ave come to me afore,' the doctor says." The man, indeed, looked just as likely as not to be laid up for six months, if not permanently crippled, as a result of his carelessness.

Yet, common as such cases are now, they were commoner when I first knew the village—when there was no cottage hospital, no proper accommodation at the workhouse infirmary, no parish nurse, and when the parish contained few people of means to help those who were in distress. I remember once looking round in that early period, and noting how there was hardly a cottage to be seen which had not, to my own knowledge, been recently visited by trouble of some sort or another. True, the troubles were not all of them of a kind that could be avoided by any precaution, for some of them arose from the death of old people. Yet in a little cottage held on a weekly tenancy death often involves the survivors of the family in more disturbance, more privation too, than it does elsewhere. Putting these cases aside, however, I could still see where, within two hundred yards of me, there had been four other deaths—one being that of an infant, and one that of a woman in child-birth. In the other two cases the victims were strong men—one, a railway worker, who was killed on the line; the other a carter, who died of injuries received in an accident with his horse. The list of lesser misfortunes included the illness of a man who broke down while at work, with hæmorrhage of the stomach, and the bad case of a bricklayer's labourer, who lay for days raving from the effects of a sunstroke. In pre-Christian times it might have been argued that the gods were offended with the people, so thickly did disasters fall upon them, but my neighbours seemed unaware of anything abnormal in the circumstances. By lifelong experience they had learned to take calamity almost as a matter of course.

For, as I said, the experience begins early. The children, the young girls, have their share of it. During those earlier years

I am recalling, a little girl of the village, who was just beginning domestic service in my household, was, within the space
of six months, personally concerned in two accidents to little
children. She came from one of half-a-dozen families whose
cottages, for a wonder in this village, stood in a row; and
amongst scraps of her talk which were repeated to me I heard
how her little brother—only five years old, but strong at throwing stones—threw at a girl playmate and knocked out one of
her eyes. That happened in the springtime. In the autumn of
the same year a mishap, if possible more shocking at the moment, befell another child in that row of cottages. A man
there one evening was trimming a low hedge. His tool was a
fag-hook—well sharpened, for he was one of the ablest men in
the village. And near by where he worked his children were
at play, the youngest of them being between three and four
years old.

As he reached over the hedge, to chop downwards at the
farther side, this little one suddenly came running dangerously
near. "Take care, ducky!" he cried. "Don't come so close,
'r else perhaps father 'll cut ye."

He gave three more strokes, and again the child ran in. The
hook fell, right across the neck. I had these particulars from a
neighbour. "If 't had bin another half inch round, the doctor
said, 'twould have bin instant death. . . . The man was
covered with blood, and all the ground, too. I was at work
when I heared of it, but I couldn't go on after that, it upset me
so. . . . And all this mornin' I can't get it out o' my mind.
There's a shiver all up that row. They be all talkin' of it. The
poor little thing en't dead this mornin', and that's all's you can
say. They bin up all night. Ne'er a one of 'em didn't go
to bed."

So far the neighbour. Later the little maidservant, who had
gone home that evening, told me: "We was passin' by at the
time—me and my older sister. . . . She run in and wrapped
a towel round its neck."

" Where, then, was the mother?"

" She was with its father. He'd fainted. So we went in. We thought p'raps we could run for the doctor. But she went herself, jest as she was," carrying the child down to the town.

As for the girl's sister, who had behaved with some aplomb, " It made her feel rather bad afterwards. She felt sick. All the floor was covered with blood." The little maidservant had a curious look, half horror, half importance, as she said this. She herself was not more than fifteen at the time.

But sickness is commoner by far than accident, and owing to the necessity the cottagers are under of doing everything for themselves, they often get into dire straits. Of some of the things that go on one cannot hear with equanimity. The people are English; bone of our bone. But we shut our eyes. I have heard of well-to-do folk in the parish who, giving of their abundance to foreign missions, deny that there is distress here at home. The most charitable explanation of that false-hood is to suppose that across their secluded gardens and into their luxurious rooms, or even to their back-doors, an average English cottager is too proud to go. Yet it is hard to under-stand how all signs of what is so constantly happening can be shut out. For myself, I have never gone out of my way to look for what I see. I have never invited confidences. The facts that come to my knowledge seem to be merely the common-places of the village life. If examples of the people's troubles were wanted, they could be provided almost endlessly, and in almost endless diversity. But there is one feature that never varies. Year after year it is still the same tale; all the extra toil, all the discomfort, or horror, or difficulty, of dealing with sickness falls immediately on the persons of the family where the sickness occurs; and it sets its cruel mark upon them, so that the signs can be seen as one goes about, in the faces of people one does not know. And the women suffer most.

One winter evening a woman came to my door to see if she could borrow a bed-rest. Her sister, she said, had been ill with pleurisy and bronchitis for a week or more, and for the last two days had been spitting a great deal of blood. The woman looked very poor; she might have been judged needlessly shabby. A needle and thread would so soon have remedied sundry defects in her jacket, which was gaping open at the seams. But her face suggested that there were excuses for her.

I have never forgotten her face, as it showed that evening, although I have since seen it looking happier. It was dull of colour—the face of an overworked and over-burdened soul; and it had a sullen expression of helplessness and resentment. The eyes were weary and pale—I fancied that trouble had faded the colour out of them. But with all this I got an impression of something dogged and unbeaten in the woman's temper. She went away with the bed-rest, apologizing for coming to borrow it. " 'Tis so bad "—those were her words—" 'tis so bad to see 'em layin' there like that, sufferin' so much pain."

I had never seen her before—for it was years ago; and, knowing no better then, I supposed her to be between forty and fifty years old. In reality, she can hardly have been thirty. It was the stress of personal service that had marred her so young. Did her jacket need mending? As I have since learnt, at that period the youngest of her family was unborn, and the oldest cannot have been more than eight or nine. Besides nursing her sister, therefore, she had several children to wait upon, as well as her husband—a man often ailing in health. For all I know she was even then, as certainly she has been since, obliged to go out working for money, so as to keep the family going; and, seeing that she was a mother, it is probable that she herself had already known the extremity of hardship.

Because, as scarcely needs saying, the principle of self-help is strained to the uttermost at time of child-birth. Then, the other members of the family have to shift for themselves as best they can, with what little aid neighbours can find time to give; and where there are young children in the cottage, it is much if they are sufficiently fed and washed. But it is the situation of the mother herself that most needs to be considered. Let me give an illustration of how she fares.

Several years ago there was a birth in a cottage very near to me. Only a few hours before it happened the woman had walked into the town to do her shopping for herself and carry home her purchases. As soon as the birth was known, a younger sister, out at service, got a week's holiday, so that she might be at hand to help, though there was no spare room in the cottage where she could sleep. During that week, also, the parish nurse came in daily, until more urgent cases occupied all her time. After that the young mother was left to her own resources. According to someone I know, who looked in from time to time, she lay in bed with her new-born baby, utterly alone in the cottage, her husband being away at work all day for twelve hours, while the elder children were at school. She made no complaint, however, of being lonely; she thought the solitude good for her. But she was worried by thinking of the fire in the next room—the living-room, which had the only fireplace in the house, there being none in her bedroom—lest it should set fire to the cottage while she lay helpless. It seems that the hearth was so narrow and the grate so high that coals were a little apt to fall out on to the floor. Once, she said, there had almost been " a flare-up." It was when she was still getting about, and she had gone no farther away than into her garden to feed the fowls; but in that interval a coal fell beyond the fender, and she, returning, found the place full of smoke and the old hearthrug afire. The dread that this might happen again distressed her now as she lay alone, unable to move.

I could furnish more pitiful tales than this, if need were—tales of women in child-bed tormented with anxiety because their husbands are out of work, and there is no money in the cottage, and no prospect of any; or harassed by the distress of little children who miss the help which the mother cannot give, and so on. But this case illustrates the normal situation. Here there was no actual destitution, nor any fear of it, and the other children were being cared for. The husband was earning a pound a week at constant work, and the circumstances of the family were on the whole quite prosperous. But one of the conditions of prosperity was that the father of the family should be away all day, leaving the mother and infant unattended.

From whatever sickness the woman suffers, there is always the same piteous story to be told—she is destitute of help. The household drudge herself, she has no drudges to wait upon her. The other day I was told of a woman suffering from pleurisy. Her husband had left home at six o'clock for his work; a neighbour-woman came in to put on a poultice and make things comfortable; then she, too, had to go to her work. In the afternoon a visitor, looking in by chance, found that the sick woman had been alone for five hours; she was parched with thirst, and her poultice had gone cold. For yet one more example. I mentioned just now a man who was killed on the railway. His widow, quite a young woman then, reared her three or four children, earning some eight or nine shillings a week at charing or washing for people in the town; and still she keeps herself, pluckily industrious. There is one son living with her—an errand-boy—and there are two daughters both in service at a large new house in the village. During last spring the woman had influenza, and had to take to her bed, her girls being permitted to take turns in coming home to care for her. Just as she, fortunately, began to recover, this permission was withdrawn : both girls were wanted in " their place," because a young lady there had taken influenza. So they had to forsake their mother. But by-and-by one of these girls took the infection. Her " place," then, was thought to be—at home. She was sent back promptly to her mother, and it was not long before the mother herself broke down again, not being yet strong enough to do sick-nursing in addition to her daily work.

It must be borne in mind that these acute and definite troubles spring up from the surface of an ill-defined but chronic anxiety, from which very few of the cottagers are free for any length of time. For though there is not much extreme destitution, a large number of the villagers live always on the brink of it; they have the fear of it always in sight. In a later chapter I shall give some particulars as to their ways and means; in this, I only wish it to be remembered that the question of ways and means is a life-and-death one for the labourer and his wife, and leaves them little peace and little hope of it. During the trade depression which culminated in 1908-09 I was frequently made aware of the disquiet of their minds by the scraps of talk which reached me as I passed along the road, and were not meant for my hearing. From women who were comparing notes with one another, this was the sort of thing one would hear : " 'En't had nothin' to do this six weeks; and don't sim no likelihoods of it." " I *s'pose* we shall get through, somehow." " I'm sure I dunno what 'tis a-comin' to." " 'Tis bad 'nough now, in the summer; what it'll be like in the winter Gawd only knows." Again and again I heard talk like this.

And all this was only an accentuation or a slight increase in volume of a note of apprehension which in better times still runs less audibly as a kind of undertone to the people's thought. I had stopped one day to say good-morning to an old widow-woman outside her cottage. She was the mother of that young man whose funeral was mentioned two chapters back; but this was before his death, and while, in fact, he was still d ɪng a little occasional work. She spoke cheerfully, smiled even, until some chance word of mine (I have forgotten what it was) went through the armour of her fortitude, and she began to cry. Then she told me of the position she was in, and the hopelessness of it, and her determination to hold out. Some charitable lady had called upon her. " Mrs. Curtis," the lady had said, " if ever you are ill, I hope you'll be sure and send to *me*." And Mrs. Curtis had replied : " Well, ma'am, if ever I sends, you may be sure I *am* ill." " But," she added, "they don't understand. 'Tis when you're on yer feet that help's wanted—

not wait till 'tis too late." With regard to her present circumstances—she "didn't mind saying it to me—sometimes she didn't hardly know how they was goin' on," for she hadn't a penny except what her son could earn. And "people seemed to think it didn't matter for a single chap to be out o' work. They didn't think he might have a mother to keep, or, if he was in lodgin's, he couldn't live there for nothin'. . . . Sometimes we seems to be gettin' on a little, and then you has bad luck, and there you are again where you was before. It's like gettin' part way up a hill and fallin' down to the bottom again, and you got it all to begin over again."

I said something—some platitude—turning to go away. Then she managed to smile—a shining-eyed smile—saying : "Well, 'tis only for life. If 'twas for longer than that I don't know if we should hardly be able to bear it."

This was but one old woman. Yet, if you have an ear for a folk-saying, you will recognize one there in that "only for life" of hers. Be sure that a byword so compact as that was not one old woman's invention. To acquire such brevity and smoothness, it must have been wandering about the parish for years; and when it reached me at last it had been polished by the despair of hundreds of other people, as a coin is polished by passing through hundreds of hands.

V

DRINK

IT will be understood, from what was said on the subject in the first chapter, that the village population has its rough element, and that drunkenness, or at any rate excessive drinking, is very common. It is true that there are very few habitual drunkards in the parish—there are not even many men, perhaps, who frequently take too much; but, on the other hand, the majority are beer-drinkers, and every now and then one or another of them, normally sober, oversteps the limit. Thus, possibly, every other family has had its passing experience of what drunkenness means in the temporary lapse of father, or son, or brother. A rainy Bank Holiday invariably leads to much mischief in this way, and so does a sudden coming of hot weather in the summer. The men have too much to do to spare time for the public-house in the ordinary weekdays, but on Saturday and Sunday night, when the strain is relaxed, they are apt to give way too far.

The evils of drunkenness, however, are well enough known, and I do not propose to dwell on that side of the matter. But there is another aspect of it which must be considered, if only because it is so thoroughly characteristic of the old village outlook. Incidentally, this other aspect may be worth a little attention from temperance reformers.

For the truth is that the average villager's attitude towards drink and temperance is not that of an unrepentant or rebellious sinner; rather, it is the attitude of a man who has sound reasons for adhering to his own point of view. If he grows restive under the admonitions of the pharisaical, if he meets them defiantly, or if he merely laughs, as often as not it is because he feels that his mentors do not understand the situation so well as he does. How should they, who see it wholly from the outside—they who never go near the public-house; they who have no experience either of poverty or of hard work —how should they, who speak from prejudice, be entitled to dictate to him, who has knowledge? He resents the interference, considers it insulting, and goes his own way, supported by a village opinion which is entirely on his side, and certainly has its claims to respect. It is this village opinion which I wish to examine now.

In the eyes of the older villagers or of the more old-fashioned ones mere occasional drunkenness is a very venial fault. The people make a distinction between the habitual drunkard and him who occasionally drinks too much, and they are without compassion for the former. He is a " low blackguard "; they look reproachfully if you talk of trying to help him by giving him a job of work, or at any rate they pity your wasted efforts. But for the occasional defaulter they have a friendly feeling, unless, of course, he turns savage in his cups. As long as he is cheerful he is rather a figure of fun to them than anything, or he is an object of wondering interest. On a certain August Bank Holiday I saw one of our villagers staggering up the hill —a middle-aged man, far gone in drink, so that all the road was none too wide for him. Other wayfarers accompanied and observed him with a philosophically detached air, and between whiles a woman grabbed at his coat between the shoulders, trying to steady him. But by and by, lurching free, he wobbled across the road to within an inch of a perambulator with two children which another man was pushing. The drunken man leant over it, poised like an impending fate, and so hung for a few seconds before he staggered away, and it might be supposed that at least the man with the perambulator would be indignant. But not he. He merely remarked wonderingly : " You wouldn't ha' thought it possible he could ha' done it, would ye?" The other wayfarers laughed lightly, amongst them a young married woman with a refined face.

While the comic side of a man in drink makes its strong appeal to the village folk, they are ready to see excuses for him, too. Anybody, they argue, is liable to be overtaken before he knows, and where is the great disgrace in an accident that may befall themselves, or me, or you? There is at least no superiority in their outlook, no pharisaism. Listen, for proof of it, to a talk of Bettesworth's about a neighbour who had been working with the " ballast-train " on the railway all night. "You," he began—and this first word showed how innocent he was of shame in his own attitude, since he supposed that I must share

his amusement—" you'd ha' laughed if you'd ha' sin Isaac
yest'day. He was got fair boozed; an' comin' up the gully,
thinkin' he was goin' straight for 'ome, he run his head right
into they bushes down by ol' Dame Smith's. Then he got up
the slope about a dozen yards, an' begun to go back'ards 'till
he come to Dame Smith's wall, and that turn'd 'n, and he
begun to go back'ards again down the gully. I did laugh. He
bin at work all night on the ballast-train, an' come back reg'lar
fagged out, an' hadn't had no vittles—an' a feller *wants* something—and then the fust glass he has do's for 'n. He bin
workin' every night for a week, an' Sundays, too. And Alice "
(" Alice " is Isaac's wife) " is away hop-tyin' all day, so, of
course, Isaac didn't care 'bout goin' 'ome to lop about there by
hisself. . . . I've seed a many go like that. They works all
night, an' gets reg'lar fagged out, an' then the fust drop does
'em. When Alice come 'ome, she looked at least to find the
kettle boilin'. 'Stead o' that, she couldn't git in. At least, she
had to fetch the key from where she put 'n when she went away
in the mornin'. I laughed at her when I went down 'ome.
'Where is he now?' I says. ' Ah, you may laugh,' she says,
' but I got to rouse 'n up about ten o'clock an' git 'n a cup o'
tea. He got to be at work again at eleven.' That's how they
do's. Begins about ten or eleven o'clock, and don't leave off
again afore six or seven, or p'raps nine or ten, next mornin'.
Makes days an' quarters for three an' ninepence. I've knowed
a many like that come 'ome an' git boozed fust glass, like old
Isaac. I did laugh, though, and so did Dame Smith when she
was a-tellin' of me."

Inheriting from their forefathers such an unimaginative point
of view, most of the cottage folk have been, until quite lately,
far from regarding the public-house as a public nuisance. It
had a distinct value in their scheme of living. That fact was
demonstrated plainly in an outburst of popular feeling some
years ago. The licensing magistrates of the neighbourhood

had taken the extreme, and at that time unprecedented, course of refusing to renew the licenses of several houses in the town. But while the example they had thus set was winning them applause all up and down England, they were the objects, in this and the adjacent villages, of all sorts of vituperation on account of what the cottagers considered a wanton insult to their class. It must be admitted that the action of the justices had some appearance of being directed against the poor. Nobody could deny, for instance, that the houses frequented by middle-class clients, and responsible for a good deal of middle-class drinking, were all passed over, and that those singled out for extinction served only the humblest and least influential. My neighbours entertained no doubts upon the matter. They were not personally concerned—at any rate, the public-houses in this village were left open for them to go to—but the appearance of favouritism offended them. They were as sure as if it had been officially proclaimed that the intention was to impose respectability upon them against their will; their pleasures were to be curtailed to please fanatics who understood nothing and cared less about the circumstances of cottage folk. So, during some weeks the angry talk went round the village; it was not difficult to know what the people were thinking. They picked to pieces the character of the individual magistrates, planning ineffective revenge. "That old So-and-So" (Chairman of the Urban Council)—"they'd bin to his shop all their lives, but he'd find he'd took his last shillin' from 'em now! And that What's-his-Name—the workin' classes had voted for 'n at last County Council election, and this was how he served 'em! He needn't trouble to put up again, when his turn was up!" Then they commiserated the suffering publicans. "Look at poor old Mrs. ——, what kept the house down Which Street—always a most well-conducted house. Nobody couldn't find no fault with it, and 'twas her livin'! Why should she have her livin' took away like that, poor old gal? . . . They sims to think nobody en't right 'xcep' jest theirselves—as if we poor people could live an' go on same as they do. They can 'ave their drink at 'ome, and their music, but where be we to go if they shuts up the 'ouses?" Such were the remarks I heard over and over again. It seemed to the poor that there were to be no more cakes and ale, because Malvolio was virtuous, or because their own manners were not refined enough.

In the light of subsequent political events I am prepared to believe that some of this popular indignation was engineered from the public-houses. But I do not think it required much engineering. It sounded spontaneous at the time, and considering how the villagers are placed, their resentment was not unnatural. As I have said, the public-house has its value in their scheme of living. They have no means of enjoying themselves at home, no room in their cottages for entertaining friends, and they may well ask what they are to do if the public-houses are closed to them.

One thing, at least, is sure. If the ordinary village inn were nothing but the foul drink-shop which its enemies allege, if all that it provided was an irresistible temptation to depravity, the majority of the people who resort to it now would very soon leave it alone. And the same is true of the little lowly places in the town. In the third chapter I mentioned how the village women, with their menfolk and their children, too—until the recent Act of Parliament shut the children out—would make a Saturday-night call at some public-house before going home from the weekly shopping expedition. But these are the reverse of bad women. They are honest and self-respecting mothers of families; women obviously innocent of anything approaching intemperance. I have seen them chatting outside a public-house door, and then smilingly pushing it open and going in, as happily unconscious of evil as if they were going to a mothers' meeting. They see no harm in it. They are away from home, they have far to go, and they want refreshment. But it is perfectly certain that most of them would rather drop than enter such places—for they are not afraid of fatigue—if there were risk of anything really wrong within. The labouring-class woman, as already explained, takes no hurt from a frank style of talk. She is not squeamish, but she has a very strong sense of her own honour; and if you remember how keen is the village appetite for scandal, you will perceive that there can be no fear of scandal attaching to her because of a visit to a public-house, or she would not go there. It should be noted, as evidence of a strict public opinion regulating the custom, that these same women seldom enter the public-houses in the village, and never any others save on this one occasion. They require the justification of their weekly outing, when supper is delayed, and the burden of living can be forgotten amongst friends for an hour. At other times they would consider the indulgence disgraceful; and though they enjoy it just at these times, I do not remember that I have ever seen one of them showing the least sign of having carried her enjoyment too far.

The men certainly are governed by no such severe public opinion, but are free to " get a drink " at any time without being thought the worse of by their neighbours; yet they, too, for the most part, are of good and sober character enough to prove that the village public-house cannot be so utterly given up to evil as might be supposed from the horrified talk of refined people. Not many men in this parish would tolerate a place in which they could do nothing but get drunk. It is for something else that they go to the Fox or the Happy Home. The drinking is but a pleasant incident. They despise the fellow who merely goes in to have his unsociable glass and be off again, as heartily as they dislike the habitual soaker who brings their entertainment into disfavour; and they themselves keep a rough sort of order—or they increase disorder in trying to quell it—rather than that the landlord should interfere. That loud harsh talk which one hears as one passes the public-house of an evening is not what the hyper-sensitive suppose. It does not betoken drunkenness so much as uncouth manners—the manners of neglected men who spend their lives at severe physical labour, and want a little relaxation in the evening. So far as I have seen, the usual conversation in the taproom of a country public-house is a lazy and innocent interchange of remarks, which wander aimlessly from one subject to another, because nobody wants to bother his head with thinking; or else it is a vehement discussion, in which dogmatic assertion does duty for argument and loudness for force. In either case it rests and stimulates the tired men, while the drink refreshes their throats, and it has no more necessary impropriety than the drawing-room talk of the well-to-do. In this intercourse men who do not read the papers get an inkling of the news of the day, those who have no books come into contact with other minds, opinions are aired, the human craving for fun gets a little exercise; and for topics of talk, instead of those which occupy moneyed people, who know about the theatre or the Church, or foreign travel, or golf, or the state of the poor, or the depreciation of Consols, the labourers have their gardens, and the harvest, and the horses they drive. They talk about their employers, and their work, and their wages; they dispute about county cricket or exchange notes about blight, or new buildings, or the latest public sensation; and all this in endless detail, endlessly interesting to them. So, utterly unaided by arts or any contrivances for amusement, they make entertainment for themselves. That they must make it in kindly temper, too, is obvious; for who would take part in it to be usually annoyed? And it may well be conceived that in an existence so empty of other pleasures, the pleasures to be derived from company are held precious. The scheme of living would be very desolate without that consolation, would grow very illiberal and sombre. But the public-houses at least do something to prevent this, and in clinging to them the villagers have clung to something which they need and cannot get elsewhere. It is idle to pretend that the " Institute " which was started a few years ago provides a satisfactory alternative. Controlled by people of another class, whose " respectability " is irksome, and open only to members and never to women, the Institute does not lend itself to the easy intercourse which tired men enjoy at the public-house. Its billiard-table is not for their heavy hands, used to the pick-axe and shovel; its card games interrupt their talk; its newspapers remind them that they cannot read very well, and suggest a mode of life which they are unable to share.

These reasons, I believe, prevail to keep the labouring men from patronizing the Institute more even than does its strictly teetotal policy. Or perhaps I should say, rather, that while they dislike going without their beer, they object more strongly still to the principle on which it is forbidden in the Institute. For that principle is nothing more or less than a tacit arraignment of their own point of view. It imputes evil propensities to them; it directly challenges the truth of an idea which not only have they never doubted, but which their own experience seems to them to confirm. The day-labourer really knows nothing to take the place of beer. A man who has been shovelling in a gravel-pit, or carrying bricks up a ladder, or hoeing in the fields, or carting coal, for ten hours in the day, and has, perhaps, walked six or seven miles to do it, acquires a form of thirst which no other drink he can buy will touch so coolly. Of alternatives, milk fails utterly; " minerals " are worse than unsatisfactory; tea, to serve the purpose at all, must be taken very hot, and then it produces uncomfortable sweat, besides involving the expense of a fire for its preparation. There remains cold water. But cold water in copious draughts has its drawbacks, even if it can be obtained, and that is assuming too much. In this parish, at any rate, good water was, until quite lately, a scarce commodity, and nobody cared to drink the stagnant stuff out of the tanks or water-butts which supplied most of the cottages. In short, prudence itself has seemed to recommend beer as the one drink for tired men. In their view it is the safest, and the most easily obtained, and, when obtained, it affords the most refreshment. Thus much their own experience has taught the villagers.

And they have the tradition of long generations to support them in their taste. As far back as they can remember, the strongest and ablest men, whose virtues they still recall and admire, renewed their strength with beer daily. Not labourers alone, but farmers and other employers too, whose health and prosperity were a sufficient justification of their habits, were wont to begin their morning with a glass of beer, which they took, not as a stimulant, but as a food; and the belief in it as a food was so convinced that a man denied his beer by doctor's orders was hardly to be persuaded that he was not being starved of due nourishment. Such was the esteem in which beer was held twenty years ago, nor has the belief been uprooted yet. Indeed, an opinion so sanctioned to a man, by the approval of his own father and grandfather and all the worthies he can remember, does not immediately become false to him just because it is condemned by strangers who do not know him, and who, with all their temperance, seem to him a delicate and feeble folk. He prefers his own standard of good and evil, and in sitting down to his glass he has no doubt that he is following a sensible old fashion, modestly trying to be, not a fine gentleman, but a sturdy Englishman.

On much the same principle the public-house as a place of resort is justified to the villager. I have already shown how it serves him for entertainment instead of newspaper, or book, or theatre; and here, again, he has a long-standing country tradition to support him. In spite of reformers on the one hand, and on the other hand that tendency of " the trade," which is spoiling the public-house as a place of comfortable rest by frowning upon customers who stay too long and drink too little—in spite of these discouragements, the villagers still cannot believe that what was good enough for their fathers is not good enough for themselves. It might not be equally good if they wished to be " superior persons," but for the modest needs of people like themselves they think it should serve. So they go to the public-house just as their fathers did, content to miss the approval of the cultured, so long as they can do as well as those worthies. Of course, if they ever analysed their impressions, they must often go home discerning that they had been disappointed; that the company had been dull and the comfort small; that they had got less conviviality than they wanted, and more of the drink that should have been only its excuse; but as they are never introspective, so the disappointment goes unnoticed, and leads to no disillusionment.

VI

WAYS AND MEANS

BEFORE going farther I must try to give some account of the ways and means of the villagers, although, obviously, in a population so heterogeneous, nothing short of a scientific survey on the lines pursued by Sir Charles Booth or Mr. Rowntree could be of much value in this direction. The observations to be offered here pretend to no such authority. They have been collected at random, and subjected to no tests, and they refer almost exclusively to the " unskilled " labouring people.

During twenty years there have not been many fluctuations in the price of a day's labour in the parish, but probably on the whole there has been a slight increase. The increase, however, is very uncertain. While the South African War was in progress, and afterwards when Bordon Camp was building, eight miles away, labour did indeed seem to profit. But then came the inevitable trade depression, work grew scarce, and by the summer of 1909 wages had dropped to something less than they had been before the war. I heard, for instance, of a man—one of the most capable in the district—who was glad that summer to go haymaking at half a crown a day. And yet two or three years earlier he had certainly been earning from fourpence halfpenny to fivepence an hour, or, say, from three and sixpence to four shillings for a day's work. In 1909 the low-water mark was reached; the following spring saw a slight revival, and at present the average may be put at three shillings. For this sum a fairly good man can be got to do an ordinary day's work of nine hours in the vegetable-garden or at any odd job.

The builders' labourers are rather better paid—if their employment were not so intermittent—with an average of from fourpence halfpenny to fivepence an hour. Carters, too, and vanmen employed by coal-merchants, builders, and other tradesmen in the town, are comparatively well off with constant work at eighteen or twenty shillings a week. The men in the gravel-pits—but that industry is rapidly declining as one after another the pits are worked out—can earn perhaps five shillings a day if at piecework, or about three and sixpence on ordinary terms. From this sum a deduction must be made for tools, which the men provide and keep in repair themselves. It is rather a heavy item. The picks frequently need repointing, and a blacksmith can hardly do this for less than twopence the point. The gravel-work, too, is very irregular. In snow or heavy rain it has to stop, and in frost it is difficult. More than once during the winter of 1908-09, it being a time of great distress, gravel-pit workers came to me with some of those worked flints—the big paleoliths of the river-gravel—which they had found and saved up, but now desired to sell, in order to raise money for pointing their pickaxes. I have wondered sometimes if the savages who shaped those flints had ever looked out upon life so anxiously as these neighbours of mine, whose iron tools were so strangely receiving this prehistoric help.

At one time upwards of forty men in the parish had more or less constant work on one of the " ballast-trains " which the South-Western Railway kept on the line for repairing the permanent way. The work, usually done at night and on Sundays, brought them in from eighteen to twenty-four shillings a week, according to the hours they made. I do not know how many of our men are employed on the railway now, but they are certainly fewer. Some years ago—it was when the great trade depression had already hit the parish badly, and dozens of men were out of work here—the railway-company suddenly stopped this train, and consternation spread through the village at the prospect of forty more being added to the numbers of its un-employed.

Reviewing the figures, and making allowance for short time due to bad weather, public holidays, sickness, and so on, it may be estimated that even when trade is good the average weekly wage earned by one of the village men at his recognized work is something under seventeen shillings. This, however, does not constitute quite the whole income of the family. In most cases the man's wages are supplemented by small and uncertain sums derived from the work of women and children, and from odd jobs done in the evenings, and from extra earnings in particular seasons.

Field-work still employs a few women, although every year their numbers decrease. It is miserably paid at a shilling a day, or in some cases on piecework terms which hardly work out at a higher figure. Piecework, for instance, was customary in the hop-gardens (now rapidly disappearing), where the women cut the bines and "tied" or "trained" the hops at so much per acre, providing their own rushes for the tying. At hay-making and at harvesting there is work for women; and again in the hop-gardens, when the picking is over, women are useful at clearing up the bines. They can earn money, too, at trimming swedes, picking up newly-dug potatoes, and so on; but when all is said, there are not many of them who can find work to do in the fields all the year round. At the best, bad weather often interrupts them, and the stress and hardships of the work, not to mention other drawbacks, make the small earnings from it a doubtful blessing.

A considerable number of women formerly eked out the family income by taking in washing for people in the town. Several properly equipped laundries have of late years greatly reduced this employment, but it still occupies a few. The difficulties of carrying it on are considerable, apart from the discomforts of it in a small cottage. Unless a woman has a donkey and cart, it is hard for her to get the washing from her customers' homes and carry it back again. Of the amount that can be earned at the work by a married woman, with husband and children to do for, I have no knowledge.

Charwomen, more in demand than ever as the residential character of the place grows more pronounced, earn latterly as much as two shillings a day, besides at least one substantial meal. The meal is a consideration, and obviously good for the women. In bad times, when the men and even the children go rather hungry, it often happens that the mother of the family is able to keep her strength up, thanks to the tolerable food she gets three or four days a week in the houses where she goes scrubbing and cleaning.

A few women—so few that they really need not be mentioned—earn a little at needlework, two or three of them having a small dressmaking connection amongst their cottage neighbours and with servant-girls. It will be realized that the prices which such clients can afford to pay are pitifully small.

In one or other of these ways most of the labouring class women do something to add to the earnings of their husbands, so that in prosperous times the family income may approach twenty-four shillings a week. Yet the average must be below that sum. The woman's work is very irregular, and just when her few shillings would be most useful—namely, when she has a baby or little children to care for—of course her employment stops. If not, it is unprofitable in the end; for, involving as it does some neglect of the children, as well as of the woman's own health, it leads to sickness and expenses which may impoverish the whole family for years.

With regard to the minor sources of income, I have often wondered at the eagerness of the average labourer to earn an odd shilling, and at the amount of work he will do for it, after his proper day's work is over. I know several men who frequently add two or three shillings to their week's money in this way. To give an instance of how they go on, one evening recently I was unexpectedly wanting to send a heavy parcel into the town. Going out to seek somebody who would take it, I chanced upon a man—very well known to me—who was at work within the hedge of a villa garden, where he was erecting on a pole a notice-board announcing a " sale of work " shortly to be held. He had obviously nearly done, so I proposed my errand to him. Yes; he would go as soon as he had finished what he was doing. Then, perceiving that he looked tired, I commented on the fact. He smiled. " I bin mowin' all day over there at . . .," and he mentioned a farm two or three miles distant. Still, he could go with my parcel. This was at about seven o'clock in the evening, and would mean a two-mile walk for him. The very next evening, when it was raining, I saw him in the churchyard digging a grave. " Haven't been mowing to-day, have you?" " Yes," he said cheerily. Mowing is, perhaps, the most fatiguing work a man can do, but fatigue was nothing to this man where a few shillings could be earned. His ordinary wages, I believe, are eighteen shillings a week, but during last winter he was out of work for six or eight weeks.

I have known this man, and others also, to make now and then quite a little harvest, amounting to several pounds, at the unsavoury work of cleaning out cess-pits. One man, indeed— a farm-labourer by day—had for a time a sort of trade connection in the parish for this employment, and would add the labour of two or three nights a week to that of his days; but, of course, he could not keep it up for long. It is highly-paid work, as it ought to be, but the ten shillings or so that a man may earn at it four or five times a year come rather as a welcome windfall than as a part of income upon which he can rely.

The seasonal employments are disappearing from the neighbourhood, as agriculture gives place to the residential interests. Hop-picking used to be the most notable of them, and even now, spite of the much-diminished acreage under hops, it is found necessary at the schools to defer the long holiday until September, because it would be impossible to get the children to school while the hops are being picked. For all the family goes into the gardens—all, that is to say, who have no constant work. The season now lasts some three weeks, during which a family may earn anything from two to four pounds. At this season a few of the more experienced and trustworthy men—my friend who mows, and digs graves, and runs errands is one of them—do better in the hop-kilns at "drying" than in the gardens. Theirs is an anxious, a responsible, and almost a sleepless duty. The pay for it, when I last heard, was two guineas a week, and—pleasant survival from an older mode of employment—the prudent hop-grower gives his dryers a pound at Christmas as a sort of retaining-fee. It is to be observed that failure of the crop is too frequent an occurrence. In years when there are no hops, the people feel the want of their extra money all the following winter.

Another custom, as it is all but extinct, needs only a passing mention now. No longer do large gangs of our labourers—with some of their womenfolk, perhaps—troop off "down into Sussex" for the August harvesting there, and for the hoeing that follows it; and no longer is the village enriched by the gold they used to bring back. When July is ending, perhaps two or three men, whether enticed by some dream of old harvesting joys in sight of the sea, or driven by want at home, may stray off for a few weeks; but I do not hear that their adventure is ever so prosperous nowadays as to induce others to follow suit.

Where the income of a family from the united efforts of the father and mother is still so small, every shilling that can be added to it is precious, and, consequently, the children have to begin earning as early as they may. Hence there is not much lingering at school, after the minimum age for leaving has been reached. Nay, some little boys, and here and there a little girl, will make from a shilling to half a crown a week at carrying out milk or newspapers before morning school begins, so that they go to their lessons with the first freshness taken off them by three or four miles of burdened walking. In view of the wear and tear of shoe-leather, even those parents who countenance the practice are doubtful of its economy. Still, a few of them encourage it; and though, if spread out amongst the families, these pitiful little earnings could hardly make a perceptible difference to the average income, I mention them here in order to leave no source of income unnoticed. When school-days are over, the family begins to benefit from the children's work. At fourteen years old, few of the boys are put to trades, but most of them get something to do in the town, where there is a great demand for errand-boys. Their wages start at about four shillings a week, increasing in a few years to as much as seven or eight. Then, at seventeen years old or so, the untrained youths begin to compete in the labour market with the men, taking too early, and at too small wages, to the driving of carts or even to work in the gravel-pits. The amount of help that these fellows then contribute towards the family expenses out of their twelve or fourteen shillings a week depends upon the parents, but it is something if they merely keep themselves; and I believe, though I do not certainly know, that it is customary for them to pay a few shillings for their lodging at least.

For girls leaving school there is no difficulty in finding, as they say, "a little place" for a start in domestic service; for even the cheaper villas which have sprung up around the town generally need their cheap drudges. Hence, at an earlier age than the boys, the girls are taken off their parents' hands and become self-supporting. True, it is long before they can earn much more in money than suffices for their own needs in clothes and boots—they cannot send many shillings home to their mothers; but no doubt a family may be found here and there enriched to the extent of a pound or two a year by the labour of the girls.

Putting the various items together, it might seem that in favourable circumstances there would be some twenty-three or twenty-four shillings a week for a family to live on all the year round. But it must be remembered, first, that the circumstances seldom remain favourable for many months together; and, second, that the greater number of families have to do without those small supplementary sums provided by the work of children, or by odd jobs, or by the good wages of hop-drying, and so forth. Nor is this the only deduction to be made. As I have already explained, in the cases where money is most needed—namely, where there is a family of little children—the mother cannot go out to work, and the income is reduced to the bare amount earned by the father alone. And these cases are very plentiful, while, on the contrary, those in which the best conditions prevail are very scarce. Taking the village all through, and balancing bad times against good ones, I question if the income of the labouring class families averages twenty shillings a week; indeed, I should be greatly surprised to learn that it amounted to so much. In very many instances eighteen shillings or even less would be the more correct estimate.

One other item remains to be recognized, although its value is too variable to be computed with any exactness in money and added to the sum of an average week's income. What is the worth to a labourer of the crops he grows in his garden? It depends, obviously, on the man's skill, and the size of the garden, and the clemency of the seasons—matters, all of them, in which any attempt at generalization must be received with suspicion. All that can be said with certainty is that most of the cottagers are diligent to cultivate them. But when the circumstances are considered, it will be plain that the value of the produce must not be put very high. The amount of ground that can be worked in the spring and summer evenings is, after all, not much; it is but little manure that can be bought out of a total money-income of eighteen shillings a week; and even good seed is, for the same reason, seldom obtained. The return for the labour expended, therefore, is seldom equal to what it should be, and we may surmise that he is a fortunate man, or an unusually industrious one, who can make his gardening worth more than two shillings a week to him in food. There must be many cottages in the valley where the yield of the garden is scarcely half that value.

To complete the picture of the people's ways and means, it ought next to be shown how the money income is spent by an average family. To do that, however, would be beyond my power, even if it were possible to determine what an " average family " is. I know, of course, that rent takes from three and sixpence a week for the poorest hovels to six shillings for the newer tenements on the outskirts of the parish; in other words, that from a quarter to a third of the labourer's whole income goes back immediately into the pockets of the employing classes for shelter alone. I know also that payments into benefit societies drain away another eightpence to a shilling a week. I realize that very often the weekly bread bill runs away with nearly half the money that is left, and so I can reckon that tea and groceries, boots and clothes, firing and light, have somehow to be obtained at a cost of no more than seven or eight shillings weekly. But these calculations fail to satisfy me. They leave unsolved the problem of those last seven or eight shillings, on the expenditure of which turns the really vital question which an inquiry like this ought to settle. How do the people make both ends meet? Are the seven shillings as a rule enough for so many purposes? or almost, but not quite enough? or nothing like enough? After all, I do not know. Information breaks down just at this point where information is most to be desired.

There is no doubt at all, however, as to the strain and stress of the general struggle to live in the valley, the sheer wear and tear of temper and spirits involved in the daily grappling with that problem. Everywhere one comes across symptoms of it—partial evidences—but the most complete exposition that I have had was given, some years ago now, by a woman who had no intention of complaining. She came to me with a message from a neighbour who was ill, but, in explanation of her part in helping him, she began to speak of her own affairs. With some of these affairs I was already acquainted. Thus I knew her to be the mother of an exceptionally large family, so that her case could not be quite typical. But I also knew that her husband had been in constant work for many years, so that, in her case, there had been no period when the income at her disposal ceased altogether, as in the case of so many other women otherwise less handicapped than she. I was aware, too, that she herself helped out the family earnings by taking in washing.

To these items of vague knowledge she added a few particulars. As to income, I learnt that her husband—a labourer on a farm some three miles away—earned fifteen shillings a week during the winter, and rather more in the summer months, when he was allowed to do " piece-work." The piece-work had the further advantage of permitting him to begin so early in the day—four o'clock was his time in summer—that he usually got home again by four in the afternoon, and was able to do better than most men with his garden. Amongst other things, he raised flowers for sale. He was wont to send to a well-known nursery in Norfolk for his seeds—china-asters and stocks were his speciality—and he reared his plants under a little glass " light " which he had made for himself out of a few old window-sashes. His pains with these flowers were unsparing. Neighbours laughed at him (so his wife assured me, with some pride) because he went to the plants down on his hands and knees, smoking each one with tobacco to clear it from green aphis. He also raised fifty or sixty sticks of celery every year, which sold for threepence apiece. Meanwhile he by no means neglected his main business as a cottage-gardener

—namely, the growing of food-crops for home use. By renting for five shillings a year an extra plot of ground near his cottage, he was able to keep his large family supplied with potatoes for quite half the year. It was much to do. They wanted nearly a bushel of potatoes a week, the wife said; and if that was so, the man was adding, in the shape of potatoes at half a crown a bushel, the value of more than three pounds a year to his income. No doubt he grew other vegetables too—parsnips, carrots, turnips, and some green-stuff—but these were not mentioned. A little further help was at last coming from the family, the eldest daughter having begun to pay half the rent out of her earnings as a servant-girl.

Help certainly must have been welcome. There were two other girls in service, and therefore off their parents' hands; but six children—the youngest only a few months old—were still at home, dependent on what their father and mother could earn. Of these, the eldest was a boy near thirteen. " I shall be glad when he's schoolin's over," the mother said; and she had applied for a " labour certificate " which would allow him to finish school as a " half-timer," and to go out and earn a little money.

Since their marriage, twenty-three years earlier, the couple had occupied always the same cottage, at a rental of three shillings a week. After the first twenty years—the property then changing owners—the first few repairs in all that long period had been undertaken. That is to say, the outside woodwork was painted; a promise was given to do up the interior; the company's water was laid on; and—the rent was raised to three-and-sixpence. The woman thought this a hardship; but she said that her husband, looking at the bright side of things, rejoiced to think that now the water from the old tank, hitherto so precious for household uses, might be spared for his flowers.

After the rent was paid—with the daughter's help—there were about fourteen shillings left. But the man was an " Oddfellow," and his subscription was nine shillings a quarter, or eightpence halfpenny a week. In prudence, that amount should perhaps have been put by every week, but apparently prudence often had to give way to pressing needs. " When the club money's due, that's when we finds it wust," the woman re-marked. "Sometimes I've said to 'n, ' I dunno how we be goin' to git through the week.' ' Oh,' he says, ' don't you worry. We shall get to the end of 'n somehow.' "

But she did not explain, nor is it easy to conceive, how it was done. For observe, the weekly bushel of potatoes did not feed the family, even for half the year. " A gallon of potatoes a day, that's what it is," she had said; and then she had enumerated other items. " A gallon of bread a day," was needed too, besides a gallon of flour once a week " for puddings." In other words, bread and flour cost upwards of six shillings weekly. Seeing that this left but eight shillings for eight people, it is small wonder that the club-money was rarely put by, and great wonder how the family managed at all when the club-money was wanted in a lump. It must have been that they went short that week. For instance, they would do without puddings, and so save on flour and firing; and the man would forego his tobacco—he had never any time to visit the public-house, so that there was nothing to be saved in that direction. Yet assuming all this, and assuming that the eldest daughter ad-vanced a few extra shillings, still the situation remains baffling. On what could they save, out of eight shillings? Probably one or other of the children, or may be the mother herself, would make an old pair of boots serve just one more week, until there was money in hand again; and that would go far to tide the family over. Yet the next week would then have to be a pinched one; for, said the woman, " boots is the wust of all. It wants a new pair for one or t'other of us purty near every week."

So far this woman's testimony. It is corroborated by what other cottagers have told me. A man said, looking fondly at his children : " I has to buy a new pair o' shoes for one or other

of us every week. Or if I misses one week, then next week I
wants two pair." Others, again, have told of spending five to
six shillings a week on bread. But of the less essential items
one never hears. Even of clothes there is rarely any talk, and
of coal not often; nor yet often of meat, or groceries. I do not
suggest that meat and groceries are foresworn, but it would
appear that they come second in the household expenses. They
are luxuries, only to be obtained if and when more necessary
things have been provided. With regard to firing—a little coal
is made to go a long way in the labourer's cottage; and with
regard to clothes—it is doubtful if anything new is bought, in
many families, from year's end to year's end. At "rummage
sales," for a few pence, the women are now able to pick up
surprising bargains in cast-off garments, which they adapt as
best they can for their own or their children's wear. Economies
like this, however, still hardly suffice to explain how the scanty
resources are really spread out. Apart from a few cases of
palpable destitution, it is not obvious that any families in the
village suffer actual want; and seeing that inquiries in the
school in recent winters have failed to discover more than two
or three sets of children manifestly wanting food, one is led to
conclude that acute poverty is of rare occurrence here. On the
other hand, all the calculations suggest that a majority perhaps
of the labouring folk endure a less intense but chronic poverty,
in which, at some point or other every day, the provision for
bare physical needs falls a little short.

VII

GOOD TEMPER

In view of their unpromising circumstances the people as a rule
are surprisingly cheerful. It is true there are never any signs in
the valley of that almost festive temper, that glad relish of life,
which, if we may believe the poets, used to characterize the
English village of old times. Tested by that standard of happiness, it is a low-spirited, mirthless, and all but silent population
that we have here now. Of public and exuberant enjoyment
there is nothing whatever. And yet, subdued though they may
be, the cottagers usually manage to keep in tolerable spirits. A
woman made me smile the other day. I had seen her husband
a week earlier, and found him rheumatic and despondent; but
when I inquired how he did, she conceded, with a laugh:
" Yes, he had a bit o' rheumatism, but he's better now. He
'ad the 'ump then, too." I inferred that she regarded his dejec-
tion as quite an unnecessary thing; and this certainly is the
customary attitude. The people are slow to admit that they
are unhappy. At a " Penny Readings " an entertainer caused
some displeasure by a quite innocent joke in this connection.
Coming through the village, he noticed the sign of one of the
public-houses—The Happy Home—and invented a conundrum
which he put from the platform: " Why was this a very
miserable village?" But the answer, " Because it has only one
Happy Home in it," gave considerable offence. For we are
not used to these subtleties of language, and the point was
missed, a good many folk protesting that we have "a *lot* o'
happy homes " here.

That they should be so touchy about it is perhaps suggestive
—pitifully suggestive—of a suspicion in them that their happiness is open to question. None the less, the general impression

conveyed by the people's manners is that of a quiet and rather cheery humour, far indeed from gaiety, but farther still from wretchedness. And in matters like this one's senses are not deceived. I know that my neighbours have abundant excuses for being downhearted; and, as described in an earlier chapter, I sometimes overhear their complainings; but more often than not the evidence of voice-tones and stray words is reassuring rather than dispiriting.

Notice, for instance, the women who have done their shopping in the town early in the morning, and are coming home for a day's work. They are out of breath, and bothered with their armfuls of purchases; but nine times out of ten their faces look hopeful; there is no sound of grievance or of worry in their talk; their smiling " Good-morning " to you proves somehow that it is not a bad morning with them. One day a woman going to the town a little late met another already returning, loaded up with goods. " 'Ullo, Mrs. Fry," she laughed, " you be 'bliged to be fust, then?" " Yes; but I en't bought it *all*; I thought you'd be comin', so I left some for you." " That's right of ye. En't it a *nice mornin'*?" " Jest what we wants! My old man was up an' in he's garden . . ." The words grow indistinguishable as you get farther away; you don't hear what the " old man " was doing so early, but the country voices sound for a long time, comfortably tuned to the pleasantness of the day.

This sort of thing is so common that I seldom notice it, unless it is varied in some way that attracts attention. For instance, I could not help listening to a woman who was pushing her baby in a perambulator down the hill. The baby sat facing her, as bland as a little image of Buddha, and as unresponsive, but she was chaffing it. " Well, you *be* a funny little gal, *ben't* ye? Why, you be goin' back'ards into the town! Whoever heared tell o' such a thing—goin' to the town *back'*ards. You *be* a funny little gal!" To me it was a funny little procession, with a touch of the pathetic hidden away in it somewhere; but it bore convincing witness to happiness in at least one home in our valley.

It is not so easy to discover, or rather to point out, the corresponding evidence in the demeanour of the men, although when one knows them one is aware that their attitude towards life is quite as courageous as the women's, if not quite so playful. I confess that I rarely see them until they have put a day's work behind them; and they may be more lightsome when they start in the morning, at five o'clock or soon after it. Be that as it may, in the evenings I find them taciturn, nonchalant rather than cheerful, not much disposed to be sprightly. Long-striding and ungainly, they walk home; between six o'clock and seven you may be sure of seeing some of them coming up the hill from the town, alone or by twos and threes. They speak but little; they look tired and stern; very often there is nothing but a twinkle in their eyes to prove to you that they are not morose. But in fact they are still taking life seriously; their thoughts, and hopes too, are bent on the further work they mean to do when they shall have had their tea. For the more old-fashioned men allow themselves but little rest, and in many a cottage garden of an evening you may see the father of the family soberly at work, and liking it too If his wife is able to come and look on and chatter to him, or if he can hear her laughing with a friend in the next garden, so much the better; but he does not stop work. Impelled, as I shall show later, by other reasons besides those of economy, many of the men make prodigiously long days of it, at least during the summer months. I have known them to leave home at five or even four in the morning, walk five or six miles, do a day's work, walk back in the evening so as to reach home at six or seven o'clock, and then, after a meal, go on again in their gardens until eight or nine. They seem to be under some spiritual need to keep going; their conscience enslaves them. So they grow thin and gaunt in body, grave and very quiet in their spirits. But sullen they very rarely are. With rheumatism and " the 'ump " combined a man will sometimes grow exasperated and be heard to speak irritably, but usually it is a very amiable "Good-evening " that greets you from across the hedge where one of these men is silently digging or hoeing.

The nature of their work, shall I say, tends to bring them to quietness of soul? I hesitate to say it, because, though work upon the ground with spade or hoe has such a soothing influence upon the amateur, there is a difference between doing it for pleasure during a spare hour and doing it as a duty after a twelve hours' day, and without any prospect of holiday as long as one lives. Nevertheless it is plain to be seen that, albeit their long days too often reduce them to a state of apathy, these quiet and patient men experience no less often a compensating delight in the friendly feeling of the tool responding to their skill, and in the fine freshness of the soil as they work it, and the solace, so varied and so unfailingly fresh, of the open air. Thus much at least I have seen in their looks, and have heard in their speech. On a certain June evening when it had set in wet, five large-limbed men, just off their work on the railway, came striding past me up the hill. They had sacks over their shoulders; their clothes and boots, from working in gravel all day, were of the same yellowish-brown colour as the sacks; they were getting decidedly wet; but they looked enviably easy-going and unconcerned. As they went by me one after another, one sleepy-eyed man, comfortably smoking his pipe, vouch-safed no word or glance. But the others, with friendly side-long glance at me, all spoke; and their placid voices were full of rich contentment. " Good-night "; " Nice *rain* "; " G'd-evenin' "; and, last of all, " *This*'ll make the young taters grow!" The man who said this looked all alert, as if the blood were dancing in him with enjoyment of the rain; his eyes were beaming with pleasure. So the five passed up the hill home-wards, to have some supper, and then, perhaps, watch and listen to the rain on their gardens until it was time to go to bed.

I ought to mention, though I may hardly illustrate, one

faculty which is a great support to many of the men—I mean the masculine gift of " humour." Not playful-witted like the women, not yet apt, like the women, to refresh their spirits in the indulgence of sentiment and emotion, but rather solid and inclined to dim brooding thought, they are able to see the laughable side of their own misadventures and discomforts; and thanks to this they keep a sense of proportion, as though perceiving that if their labour accomplishes its end, it does not really matter that they get tired, or dirty, or wet through in doing it. This is a social gift, of small avail to the men work- ing alone in their gardens; but it serves them well during the day's work with their mates, or when two or three of them together tackle some job of their own, such as cleaning out a well, or putting up a fowl-house. Then, if somebody gets splashed, or knocks his knuckles, and softly swears, his wrath turns to a grin as the little dry chuckle or the sly remark from the others reminds him that his feelings are understood. It is well worth while to be present at these times. I laugh now to think of some of them that I have enjoyed; but I will not risk almost certain failure in trying to describe them, for their flavour depends on minute details into which I have no space to enter.

But whatever alleviations there may be to their troubles, the people's geniality is still noteworthy. In circumstances that contrast so pitifully with those of the employing classes, it would seem natural if they were full of bitterness and envy; yet that is by no means the case. Being born to poverty and the labouring life, they accept the position as if it were entirely natural. Of course it has its drawbacks; but they suppose that it takes all sorts to make a world, and since they are of the labouring sort they must make the best of it. With this simple philosophy they have contrived hitherto to meet their troubles calmly, not blaming other people for them, unless in individual cases, and hardly dreaming of translating them into social in- justice. They have no sense of oppression to poison their lives.

The truth which economists begin to recognize, that where there are wealthy and idle classes there must as an inevitable result be classes who are impoverished and overworked, has not found its way into the villager's head.

So, supported by an instinctive fatalism, the people have taken their plight for granted, without harbouring resentment against the more fortunate. It may be added that most of them are convinced believers in those fallacies which cluster around the phrase " making work." It were strange if they were not. The labourer lives by being employed at work; and, knowing his employer personally—this or that farmer or tradesman or villa-resident—he sees the work he lives by actually being " made." Only very rarely does it occur to him that when he goes to the shop he, too, makes work. In bad times, perhaps, he gets an inkling of it; and then, when wages are scarce, and the public-house landlord grumbles, old-fashioned villagers will say, " Ah, they misses the poor man, ye see!" But the idea is too abstract to be followed to its logical conclusion. The people do not see the multitudes at work for them in other counties, making their boots and ready-made clothes, getting their coal, importing their cheap provisions; but they do see, and know by name, the well-to-do of the neighbourhood, who have new houses built and new gardens laid out; and they naturally enough infer that labour would perish if there were no well-to-do people to be supplied.

Against the rich man, therefore, the labourers have no sort of animosity. If he will spend money freely, the richer he is the better. Throughout the south of England this is the common attitude. I remember, not long ago, on a holiday, coming to a village which looked rarely prosperous for its county, owing, I was told, to the fact that the county lunatic asylum near by caused money to be spent there. In the next village, which was in a deplorable state, and had no asylum, the people were looking enviously towards this one, and wishing that at least their absentee landlords would come and hunt the neighbourhood, though it appeared that one of these gentlemen was a Bishop. But the labouring folk were not exacting as to the sort of person —lunatics, fox-hunters, Bishops—anybody would be welcome who would spend riches in a way to "make work." And so here. This village looks up to those who control wealth as if they were the sources of it; and if there is a little dislike of some of them personally, there has so far appeared but little bitterness of feeling against them as a class.

I do not say that there has never been any grumbling. One day, years ago, an old friend of mine broke out, in his most contemptuous manner, "What d'ye think Master Dash Blank bin up to now?" He named the owner of a large estate near the town. "Bin an' promised all his men a blanket an' a quarter of a ton o' coal at Christmas. A *blanket*, and a *quarter of a ton o' coal!* Pity as somebody hadn't shoved a brick down his throat, when he *had* got 'n open, so's to *keep* 'n open!" The sentiment sounds envious, but in fact it was scornful. It was directed, not against the great man's riches, but against the well-known meanness he displayed anew in his contemptible gifts.

A faint trace of traditional class animosity sounds in one or two customary phrases of the village, for instance in the saying that there is one law for the rich and another for the poor. Yet this has become such a by-word as to be usually stated with a smile; for is it not an old acquaintance amongst opinions? The older people even have a humorous development of it. According to their improved version, there are not two only, but three kinds of law : one kind for the rich, one for the poor, and one "the law that nobody can't make." What is this last? Why, the law "to make a feller pay what en't got nothink." By such witticisms the edge of bitterness is turned; the sting is taken out of that sense of inequality which, as the labourer probably knows, would poison his present comfort and lead him into dangerous courses if he let it rankle. With one exception, the angriest recognition of class differences which I have come across amongst the villagers was when I passed two women on their way home from the town, where, I surmised, they, or some friend of theirs, had just been fined at the County Court or the Petty Sessions. "Ah!" one was saying, with spiteful emphasis, "*there'll* come a great day for they to have *their* Judge, same as we *poor* people." Yet even there, if the emotion was newly-kindled, the sentiment was too antiquated to mean much. For it is a very ancient idea—that of getting even with one's enemies in the next world instead of in this. So long as the poor can console themselves by leaving it to Providence to avenge them at the Day of Judgment, it cannot be said that there is any virulent class-feeling amongst them. The most that you can make of it is that they occasionally feel spiteful. It happened, in this case, to be against rich people that those two women felt their momentary grudge; but it was hardly felt against the rich as a class; and if the same kind of offence had come from some neighbour, they would have said much the same kind of thing. In the family disputes which occur now and then over the inheritance of a few pounds' worth of property, the losers put on a very disinterested and superior look, and say piously of the gainers : "Ah, they'll never prosper ! They *can't* prosper !"

The exceptional case alluded to above was certainly startling. I was talking to an old man whom I had long known : a little wrinkled old man, deservedly esteemed for his integrity and industry, full of experience as well as of old-world notions, sometimes a little "grumpy," a little caustic in his manner of talking, but on the whole quite kindly and tolerant in his disposition. You could often watch in his face the habitual practice of patience, as, with a wry smile and a contemptuous remark, he dismissed some disagreeable topic or other from his thoughts. He had come down in the world. His father's cottage, already mortgaged when he inherited it, had been sold over his head after the death of the mortgagee, so that thenceforth he was on no better footing than any other of the labourers.   Gradually, as the demand failed for his old-fashioned forms of skill—thatching, mowing, and so on—his position became more and more precarious; yet he remained good-tempered, in his queer acid way, until he was past seventy years old.   That evening, when he startled me, he had been telling of his day's work as a road-mender, and he was mightily philosophical over the prospect of having to give up even that last form of regular employment, because of the exposure and the miles of walking which it entailed.   Nobody could have thought him a vindictive or even a discontented man so far. By chance, however, something was said about the uncultivated land in the neighbourhood, covered as it is with fir-woods now; and at that he suddenly fired up.   Pointing to the woods, which could be seen beyond the valley, he said spitefully, while his eyes blazed: "I can remember when all that was open common, and you could go where you mind to.   Now 'tis all fenced in, and if you looks over the fence they'll lock ye up. And they en't got no more *righ*t to it, Mr. Bourne, than you and me have!   I should *like* to see they woods all go up in flames!"

That was years ago.   The woods are still flourishing; the old man is past doing any mischief; but I remember his indignation.   And it was the sole case I have met with in the parish, of animosity harboured not so much against persons as against the existing position of things.   This one man was alive to the injustice of a social arrangement; and in that respect he differed from the rest of my neighbours, unless I am much deceived in them.   Of course there may be more of envious feeling abroad in the village than I know about.   It is the sort of thing that would keep itself secret; and perhaps this old man's contemporaries, who shared his recollections, silently shared his bitterness too.   But if so, I do not believe that they have passed the feeling on to their children.   The impression is strong in me that the people have never learnt to look upon the distribution of property, which has left them so impoverished, as anything other than an inevitable dispensation of Providence. If they thought otherwise, at any rate if the contrary view were at all prevalent amongst them, they must be most gifted hypocrites, to go about with the good temper in their eyes and the cheerfulness in their voices that I have been describing.

To what should it be attributed—this power of facing poverty with contentment? To some extent doubtless it rests on Christian teaching, although perhaps not much on the Christian teaching of the present day. Present-day religion, indeed, must often seem to the cottagers a tiresome hobby reserved to the well-to-do; but from distant generations there seems to have come down, in many a cottage family, a rather lofty religious sentiment which fosters honesty, patience, resignation, courage. Much of the gravity, much of the tranquillity of soul of the more sedate villagers must be ascribed to this traditional influence, whose effects are attractive enough, in the character and outlook of many an old cottage man and woman.

Yet there is much more in the village temper than can be accounted for by this cause alone. In most of the people the cheerfulness does not suggest pious resignation, in the hope of the next world; it looks like a grim and lusty determination to make the best of this world. It is contemptuous, or laughing. As I have shown, it has a tendency to be beery. It occasionally breaks out into disorder. In fact, if the folk were not habitually overworked they would be boisterous, jolly. Of course it may all proceed from the strong English nature in them; and in that case we need seek no other explanation of it. Yet if one influence, namely, a traditional Christianity, is to be credited—as it certainly should be—with an effect upon the village character in one direction, then probably, behind this other effect in another direction, some other influence is at work. And for my part I make no doubt of it. The cheerfulness of the cottagers rests largely upon a survival of the outlook and habits of the peasant days before the common was enclosed. It is not a negative quality. My neighbours are not merely patient and loftily resigned to distress; they are still groping, dimly, for an enjoyment of life which they have not yet realized to be unattainable. They maintain the peasant spirits. Observe, I do not suggest that they are intentionally old-fashioned. I do not believe them to be sympathetic at all to those self-conscious revivals of peasant arts which are now being recommended to the poor by a certain type of philanthropists. They make no æsthetic choice. They do not deliberate which of the ancestral customs it would be " nice " for them to follow; but, other things being equal, they incline to go on in the way that has been usual in their families. It is a tendency that sways them, not a thought-out scheme of the way to live. Now and again, perhaps, some memory may strengthen the tendency, as they are reminded of this or that fine old personality worthy of imitation, or as some circumstance of childhood is recalled, which it would be pleasant to restore; but in the main the force which bears them on is a traditional outlook, fifty times more potent than definite but transient memories. This it is that has to be recognized in my neighbours. Down in the valley, until the " residents " began to flock in, the old style of thinking lingered on; in the little cottages the people, from earliest infancy, were accustomed to hear all things—persons and manners, houses and gardens, and the day's work—appraised by an ancient standard of the countryside; and consequently it happens that this evening while I am writing, out there on the slopes of the valley the men and women, and the very children whose voices I can just hear, are living by an outlook in which the values are different from those of easy-going people, and in which, especially, hardships have never been met by peevishness, but have been beaten by good-humour.

III

THE ALTERED CIRCUMSTANCES

VIII

THE PEASANT SYSTEM

THE persistence into the twentieth century—the scarcely realized persistence—not so much of any definite ideas, as of a general temper more proper to the eighteenth century, accounts for all sorts of anomalies in the village, and explains not only why other people do not understand the position of its inhabitants to-day, but why they themselves largely fail to understand it. They are not fully aware of being behind the times, and probably in many respects they no longer are so; only there is that queer mental attitude giving its bias to their view of life. Although very feebly now, still the momentum derived from a forgotten cult carries them on.

But, having noticed the persistence of the peasant traditions, we have next to notice how inadequate they are to present needs. Our subject swings round here. Inasmuch as the peasant outlook lingers on in the valley, it explains many of those peculiarities I have described in earlier chapters; but, inasmuch as it is a decayed and all but useless outlook, we shall see in its decay the significance of those changes in the village which have now to be traced out. The little that is left from the old days has an antiquarian or a gossipy sort of interest; but the lack of the great deal that has gone gives rise to some most serious problems.

For, as I hinted at the outset, the " peasant " tradition in its vigour amounted to nothing less than a form of civilization— the home-made civilization of the rural English. To the

exigent problems of life it furnished solutions of its own—
different solutions, certainly, from those which modern civilization gives, but yet serviceable enough. People could find in it
not only a method of getting a living, but also an encourage-
ment and a help to live well. Besides employment there was an
intense interest for them in the country customs. There was
scope for modest ambition too. Best of all, those customs provided a rough guidance as to conduct—an unwritten code to
which, though we forget it, England owes much. It seems
singular to think of now; but the very labourer might reason-
ably hope for some satisfaction in life, nor trouble about
"raising" himself into some other class, so long as he could
live on peasant lines. And it is in the virtual disappearance of
this civilization that the main change in the village consists.
Other changes are comparatively immaterial. The valley might
have been invaded by the leisured classes; its old appearance
might have been altered; all sorts of new-fangled things might
have been introduced into it; and still under the surface it
would have retained the essential village characteristics, had but
the peasant tradition been preserved in its integrity amongst
the lowlier people; but with that dying, the village, too, dies
where it stands. And that is what has been happening here. A
faint influence from out of the past still has its feeble effect;
but, in this corner of England at least, what we used to think
of as the rural English are, as it were, vanishing away—vanishing as in a slow transformation, not by death or emigration,
not even by essential change of personnel, but by becoming
somehow different in their outlook and habits. The old
families continue in their old home; but they begin to be a new
people.

It was of the essence of the old system that those living under
it subsisted in the main upon what their own industry could
produce out of the soil and materials of their own countryside.
A few things, certainly, they might get from other neighbour-
hoods, such as iron for making their tools, and salt for curing

their bacon; and some small interchange of commodities there was, accordingly, say between the various districts that yielded cheese, and wool, and hops, and charcoal; but as a general thing the parish where the peasant people lived was the source of the materials they used, and their wellbeing depended on their knowledge of its resources. Amongst themselves they would number a few special craftsmen—a smith, a carpenter or wheelwright, a shoemaker, a pair of sawyers, and so on; yet the trades of these specialists were only ancillary to the general handiness of the people, who with their own hands raised and harvested their crops, made their clothes, did much of the building of their homes, attended to their cattle, thatched their ricks, cut their firing, made their bread and wine or cider, pruned their fruit-trees and vines, looked after their bees, all for themselves. And some at least, and perhaps the most, of these economies were open to the poorest labourer. Though he owned no land, yet as the tenant, and probably the permanent tenant, of a cottage and garden he had the chance to occupy himself in many a craft that tended to his own comfort. A careful man and wife needed not to despair of becoming rich in the possession of a cow or a pig or two, and of good clothes and household utensils; and they might well expect to see their children grow up strong and prosperous in the peasant way.

Thus the claim that I have made for the peasant tradition—namely, that it permitted a man to hope for well-being without seeking to escape from his own class into some other—is justified, partially at least. I admit that the ambition was a modest one, but there were circumstances attending it to make it a truly comforting one too. Look once more at the conditions. The small owners of the parish might occupy more land than the labourers, and have the command of horses and waggons, and ploughs and barns, and so on; but they ate the same sort of food and wore the same sort of clothes as the poorer folk, and they thought the same thoughts too, and talked in the same dialect, so that the labourer working for them was not oppressed by any sense of personal inferiority. He might even excel in some directions, and be valued for his excellence. Hence, if his ambition was small, the need for it was not very great.

And then, this life of manifold industry was interesting to live. It is impossible to doubt it. Not one of the pursuits I have mentioned failed to make its pleasant demand on the labourer for skill and knowledge; so that after his day's wage-earning he turned to his wine-making or the management of his pigs with the zest that men put into their hobbies. Amateurs the people were of their homely crafts—very clever amateurs, too, some of them. I think it likely, also, that normally even wage-earning labour went as it were to a peaceful tune. In the elaborate tile-work of the old cottage roofs, in the decorated ironwork of decrepit farm-waggons, in the carefully fashioned field-gates—to name but a few relics of the sort—many a village of Surrey and Hampshire and Sussex has ample proofs that at least the artisans of old time went about their work placidly, unhurriedly, taking time to make their products comely. And probably the same peaceful conditions extended to the labouring folk. Of course, their ploughing and harvesting have left no traces; but there is much suggestiveness in some little things one may note, such as the friendly behaviour of carter-men to their horses, and the accomplished finish given to the thatch of ricks, and the endearing names which people in out-of-the-way places still bestow upon their cows. Quietly, but convincingly, such things tell their tale of tranquillity, for they cannot have originated amongst a people habitually unhappy and harassed. But whether the day's work went comfortably or no, certainly the people's own home-work—to turn to that again—must often have been agreeable, and sometimes delightful. The cottage crafts were not all strictly useful; some had simple æsthetic ends. If you doubt it, look merely at the clipped hedges of box and yew in the older gardens; they are the result of long and loving care, but they serve no particular end, save to please the eye. So, too, in general, if you think that the folk of old were inappreciative of beauty, you have but to listen to their names of flowers—sweet-william, hearts-ease, marigold, meadow-sweet, night-shade—for proof that English peasant-life had its graceful side.

Still, their useful work must, after all, have been the main-stay of the villagers; and how thoroughly their spirits were immersed in it I suppose few living people will ever be able to realize. For my part, I dare not pretend to comprehend it; only at times I can vaguely feel what the peasant's attitude must have been. All the things of the countryside had an intimate bearing upon his own fate; he was not there to admire them, but to live by them—or, say, to wrest his living from them by familiar knowledge of their properties. From long experience —experience older than his own, and traditional amongst his people—he knew the soil of the fields and its variations almost foot by foot; he understood the springs and streams; hedgerow and ditch explained themselves to him; the coppices and woods, the water-meadows and the windy heaths, the local chalk and clay and stone, all had a place in his regard—reminded him of the crafts of his people, spoke to him of the economies of his own cottage life; so that the turfs or the faggots or the timber he handled when at home called his fancy while he was hand-ling them, to the landscape they came from. Of the intimacy of this knowledge, in minute details, it is impossible to give an idea. I am assured of its existence because I have come across surviving examples of it, but I may not begin to describe it. One may, however, imagine dimly what the cumulative effect of it must have been on the peasant's outlook; how attached he must have grown—I mean how closely linked—to his own countryside. He did not merely " reside " in it; he was part of it, and it was part of him. He fitted into it as one of its native denizens, like the hedgehogs and the thrushes. All that hap-pened to it mattered to him. He learnt to look with reverence upon its main features, and would not willingly interfere with their disposition. But I lose the best point in talking of the

individual peasant; these things should rather be said of the
tribe—the little group of folk—of which he was a member. As
they, in their successive generations, were the denizens of their
little patch of England—its human fauna—so it was with
traditional feelings derived from their continuance in the land
that the individual peasant man or woman looked at the fields
and the woods.

Out of all these circumstances—the pride of skill in handi-
crafts, the detailed understanding of the soil and its materials,
the general effect of the well-known landscape, and the faint
sense of something venerable in its associations—out of all this
there proceeded an influence which acted upon the village
people as an unperceived guide to their conduct, so that they
observed the seasons proper for their varied pursuits almost as
if they were going through some ritual. Thus, for instance, in
this parish, when, on an auspicious evening of spring, a man
and wife went out far across the common to get rushes for the
wife's hop-tying, of course it was a consideration of thrift that
sent them off; but an idea of doing the right piece of country
routine at the right time gave value to the little expedition.
The moment, the evening, became enriched by suggestion of
the seasons into which it fitted, and by memories of years gone
by. Similarly in managing the garden crops : to be too late, to
neglect the well-known signs which hinted at what should be
done, was more than bad economy; it was dereliction of peasant
duty. And thus the succession of recurring tasks, each one of
which seemed to the villager almost characteristic of his own
people in their native home, kept constantly alive a feeling that
satisfied him and a usage that helped him. The feeling was
that he belonged to a set of people rather apart from the rest of
the world—a people necessarily different from others in their
manners, and perhaps poorer and ruder than most, but yet
fully entitled to respect and consideration. The usage was just
the whole series or body of customs to which his own people
conformed; or, more exactly, the accepted idea in the village of

D

what ought to be done in any contingency, and of the proper way to do it. In short, it was that unwritten code I spoke of just now—a sort of *savoir vivre*—which became part of the rural labourer's outlook, and instructed him through his days and years. It was hardly reduced to thoughts in his consciousness, but it always swayed him. And it was consistent with—nay, it implied—many strong virtues: toughness to endure long labour, handiness, frugality, habits of early rising. It was consistent too—that must be admitted—with considerable hardness and " coarseness " of feeling; a man might be avaricious, loose, dirty, quarrelsome, and not offend much against the essential peasant code. Nor was its influence very good upon his intellectual development, as I shall show later on. Yet whatever its defects, it had those qualities which I have tried to outline; and where it really flourished it ultimately led to gracefulness of living and love of what is comely and kindly. You can detect as much still, in the flavour of many a mellow folk-saying, not to mention folk-song; you may divine it yet in all kinds of little popular traits, if once you know what to look for.

In this particular valley, where the barren soil challenged the people to a severer struggle for bare subsistence, the tradition could not put forth its fairer, its gentler, features; nevertheless the backbone of the village life was of the genuine peasant order. The cottagers had to " rough it," to dispense with softness, to put up with ugliness; but by their own skill and knowledge they forced the main part of their living out of the soil and materials of their own neighbourhood. And in doing this they won at least the rougher consolations which that mode of life had to offer. Their local knowledge was intensely interesting to them; they took pride in their skill and hardihood; they felt that they belonged to a set of people not inferior to others, albeit perhaps poorer and ruder; and all the customs which their situation required them to follow sustained their belief in the ancestral notions of good and evil. In other words, they had a civilization to support them—a poor thing, perhaps, a poor kind of civilization, but their own, and entirely within the reach of them all. I have no hesitation in affirming all this; because, though I never saw the system in its completeness, I came here soon enough to find a few old people still partially living by it. These old people, fortunate in the possession of their own cottages and a little land, were keepers of pigs and donkeys, and even a few cows. They kept bees, too; they made wine; they often paid in kind for any services that neighbours did for them; and with the food they could grow, and the firing they could still obtain from the woods and heath, their living was half provided for. The one of them I knew best was not the most typical. Shrewd old man that he was, he had adapted himself so far as suited him to a more commercial economy, and had grown suspicious and avaricious; yet if he could have been translated suddenly back into the eighteenth century, he would scarce have needed to change any of his habits, or even his clothes. He wore an old-fashioned " smock frock," doubt-less home-made; and in this he pottered about all day—pot-tered, at least, in his old age, when I knew him—not very spruce as to personal cleanliness, smelling of his cow-stall, saving money, wanting no holiday, independent of books and newspapers, indifferent to anything that happened farther off than the neighbouring town, liking his pipe and glass of beer, and never knowing what it was to feel dull. I speak of him because I knew him personally; but there were others of whom I used to hear, though I never became acquainted with them, who seem to have been hardly at all tainted with the com-mercial spirit, and were more in the position of labourers than this man, yet lived almost dignified lives of simple and self-supporting contentment. Of some of them the middle-aged people of to-day still talk, not without respect.

But in writing of such folk I have most emphatically to use the past tense; for although a sort of afterglow from the old civilization still rests upon the village character, it is fast fading out, and it has not much resemblance to the genuine thing of half a century ago. The direct light has gone out of the people's life—the light, the meaning, the guidance. They have no longer a civilization, but only some derelict habits left from that which has gone. And it is no wonder if some of those habits seem now stupid, ignorant, objectionable; for the fitness has departed from them, and left them naked. They were acquired under a different set of circumstances—a set of circumstances whose disappearance dates from, and was caused by, the enclosure of the common.

IX

THE NEW THRIFT

ONE usually thinks of the enclosure of a common as a procedure which takes effect immediately, in striking and memorable change; yet the event in this village seems to have made no lasting impression on people's minds. The older folk talk about things that happened " before the common was enclosed " much as they might say " before the flood," and occasionally they discuss the history of some allotment or other made under the award; but one hears little from them to suggest that the fateful ordinance seemed to them a fateful one at the time.

It may be that the stoical village temper is in part accountable for this indifference. As the arrangement was presumably made over the heads of the people, they doubtless took it in a fatalistic way as a thing that could not be helped and had better be dismissed from their thoughts. Were this all, however, I think that I should have heard more of the matter. Had sudden distress fallen upon the valley, had families been speedily and obviously ruined by the enclosure, some mention of the fact would surely have reached me. But the truth appears to be that nothing very definite or striking ensued, to be remembered. The change was hardly understood, or, at any rate, its importance was not appreciated, by the people concerned.

Perhaps, indeed, its calamitous nature was veiled at first behind some small temporary advantages which sprang from it. True, I question if the benefits experienced here were equal to those which are said to have been realized in similar circumstances elsewhere. In other parishes, where the farmers have been impoverished and the labourers out of work, the latter, at the enclosure of a common, have sometimes found welcome employment in digging out or fencing in the boundaries of the new allotments, and in breaking up the fresh ground. So the landowners say. But here, where there were few men wanting constant labour, the opportunity of work to do was hardly called for, and the making of boundaries was in many cases neglected. In that one way, therefore, not many can have derived any profit from the enclosure. On the other hand, an advantage was really felt, I think, in the opening that arose for building cottages on the newly-acquired freeholds. Quite a number of cottages seem to date from that period; and I infer that the opportunity was seized by various men who wished to provide new house-room for themselves, or for a married son or daughter. They could still go to work almost on the old lines. Perhaps the recognized price—seventy pounds, it is said to have been, for building a cottage of three rooms—would have to be exceeded a little, when timbers for floor and roof could no longer be had for the cutting out of fir-trees on the common; and yet there, after all, were the trees, inexpensive to buy; and there was the peasant tradition, still unimpaired, to encourage and commend such enterprise.

There is really little need, however, for these explanations of the people's unconcern at the disaster which had, in fact, befallen them. The passing of the common seemed unimportant at the time, not so much because a few short-lived advantages concealed its meaning as because the real disadvantages were slow to appear. At first the enclosure was rather a nominal event than an actual one. It had been made in theory; in practice it was deferred. I have just said that in many cases the boundaries were left unmarked; I may add now that to this day they have not quite all been defined, although the few spots which remain unfenced are not worthy of notice. They are to be found only in places where building is impossible; elsewhere all is now closed in. For it is the recent building boom that has at last caused the enclosure to take its full effect. Before that began, not more than ten or twelve years ago, there were abundant patches of heath still left open; and on many a spot where nowadays the well-to-do have their tennis or their afternoon tea, of old I have seen donkeys peacefully grazing. The donkeys have had to go, their room being wanted, and not many cottagers can keep a donkey now; but kept they were, and in considerable numbers, until these late years, in spite of the enclosure. But if the end could be deferred so long, one may judge how slowly the change began—slowly and inconspicuously, so that those who saw the beginning could almost ignore it. Even the cows—once as numerous as the donkeys—were not given up quite immediately, though in a few years they were all gone, I am told. But long after them, heath for thatching and firing might still be cut in waste places; fern continued until six or seven years ago to yield litter for pigstyes; and since these things still seemed to go on almost as well after the enclosure as before it, how should the people have imagined that their ancient mode of life had been cut off at the roots, and that it had really begun to die where it stood, under their undiscerning eyes?

Nevertheless, that was the effect. To the enclosure of the common more than to any other cause may be traced all the changes that have subsequently passed over the village. It was like knocking the keystone out of an arch. The keystone is not the arch; but, once it is gone, all sorts of forces, previously resisted, begin to operate towards ruin, and gradually the whole structure crumbles down. This fairly illustrates what has happened to the village, in consequence of the loss of the common. The direct results have been perhaps the least important in themselves; but indirectly the enclosure mattered, because it left the people helpless against influences which have sapped away their interests, robbed them of security and peace, rendered their knowledge and skill of small value, and seriously affected their personal pride and their character. Observe it well. The enclosure itself, I say, was not actually the cause of all this; but it was the opening, so to speak, through which all this was let in. The other causes which have been at work could hardly have operated as they have done if the village life had not been weakened by the changes directly due to the loss of the common.

They consisted—those changes—in a radical alteration of the domestic economy of the cottagers. Not suddenly, but none the less inevitably, the old thrift—the peasant thrift—which the people understood thoroughly had to be abandoned in favour of a modern thrift—commercial thrift—which they understood but vaguely. That was the essential effect of the enclosure, the central change directly caused by it; and it struck at the very heart of the peasant system.

For note what it involved. By the peasant system, as I have already explained, people derived the necessaries of life from the materials and soil of their own countryside. Now, so long as they had the common, the inhabitants of the valley were in a large degree able to conform to this system, the common being, as it were, a supplement to the cottage gardens, and furnishing means of extending the scope of the little home industries. It encouraged the poorest labourer to practise, for instance, all those time-honoured crafts which Cobbett, in his little book on Cottage Economy, had advocated as the one hope for labourers. The cow-keeping, the bread-making, the fattening of pigs and curing of bacon, were actually carried on here thirty years after Cobbett's time, besides other things not mentioned by him, such as turf-cutting on the heath and wheat-growing in the gardens. But it was the common that made all this possible. It was only by the spacious " turn-out " which it afforded that the people were enabled to keep cows and get milk and butter; it was only with the turf-firing cut on the common that they could smoke their bacon, hanging it in the wide chimneys over those old open hearths where none but such fuel could be used; and, again, it was only because they could get furze from the common to heat their bread ovens that it was worth their while to grow a little wheat at home and have it ground into flour for making bread. With the common, however, they could, and did, achieve all this. I am not dealing in supposition. I have mentioned nothing here that I have not learnt from men who remember the system still flourishing— men who in their boyhood took part in it, and can tell how the turfs were harvested, and how the pig-litter was got home and stacked in ricks; men who, if you lead them on, will talk of the cows they themselves watched over on the heath—two from this cottage, three from that one yonder, one more from Master Hack's, another couple from Trusler's, until they have numbered a score, perhaps, and have named a dozen old village names. It all actually happened. The whole system was " in full swing " here, within living memory. But the very heart of it was the open common.

Accordingly, when the enclosure began to be a fact, when the cottager was left with nothing to depend upon save his garden alone, as a peasant he was a broken man—a peasant shut out from his countryside and cut off from his resources. True, he might still grow vegetables, and keep a pig or two, and provide himself with pork; but there was little else that he could do in the old way. It was out of the question to obtain most of his supplies by his own handiwork: they had to be procured, ready-made, from some other source. That source, I need hardly say, was a shop. So the once self-supporting cottager turned into a spender of money at the baker's, the coal-merchant's, the provision-dealer's; and, of course, needing to spend money, he needed first to get it.

The change was momentous, as events have sufficiently proved. In the matter of earning, to be sure, the difference has appeared rather in the attitude of the people than in the actual method of going about to get money. To a greater or less extent, most of them were already wage-earners, though not regularly. If a few had been wont to furnish themselves with money in true peasant fashion—that is to say, by selling their goods, their butter, or milk, or pig-meat, instead of their labour —still, the majority had wanted for their own use whatever they could produce in this way, and had been obliged to sell their labour itself, when they required money. Wage-earning, therefore, was no new thing in the village; only, the need to earn became more insistent, when so many more things than before had to be bought with the wages. Consequently, it had to be approached in a more businesslike, a more commercial, spirit. Unemployment, hitherto not much worse than a regrettable inconvenience, became a calamity. Every hour's work acquired a market value. The sense of taking part in time-honoured duties of the countryside disappeared before the idea —so very important now—of getting shillings with which to go to a shop; while even the home industries which were still practicable began to be valued in terms of money, so that a man was tempted to neglect his own gardening if he could sell his labour in somebody else's garden. Thus undermined, the peasant outlook gave way, perforce, to that of the modern labourer, and the old attachment to the countryside was weakened. In all this change of attitude, however, we see only one of those indirect results of the enclosure of the common which were spoken of above. If the villagers became more mercenary, it was not because the fencing in of the heaths immediately caused them to become so, but because it left them helpless to resist becoming so—left them a prey to considerations whose weight they had previously not so much felt. After all, the new order of things did but intensify the need of wage-earning; it made no difference in the procedure of it.

But in regard to spending the case was otherwise. Under the old régime, although probably a small regular expenditure of money had been usual, yet in the main the peasant's expenditure was not regular, but intermittent. Getting so much food and firing by his own labour, he might go for weeks without needing more than a few shillings to make up occasional deficiencies. His purse was subject to no such constant drain as that for which the modern labourer has to provide. In short, the regular expenses were small, the occasional ones not crushing. But to-day, when the people can no longer produce for themselves, the proportion has changed. It has swung round so completely that nearly all the expenses have become regular, while those of the other sort have wellnigh disappeared. Every week money has to be found, and not only, as of old, for rent, and boots, and for some bread and flour, but also for butter or margarine, sugar, tea, bacon or foreign meat if possible, lard, jam, and—in the winter, at least—coal. Even water is an item of weekly expense; for where the company's water is laid on to a cottage, there is sixpence a week or so added to the rent. The only important thing which is still not bought regularly is clothing. The people get their clothes when they can, and when they positively must.

As a result, the former thrift of the village has been entirely subverted. For earning and spending are not the whole of economy. There is saving to be considered; and, in consequence of the turn-over of expenses from the occasional to the regular group, the cottagers have been obliged to resort to methods of saving specially adapted to the changed conditions. The point is of extreme importance. Under the old style, a man's chief savings were in the shape of commodities ready for use, or growing into use. They were, too, a genuine capital, inasmuch as they supported him while he replaced and increased them. The flitches of bacon, the little stores of flour and home-made wine, the stack of firing, the small rick of fern or grass, were his savings-bank, which, while he drew from it daily, he replenished betimes as he planted his garden, and brought home heath and turf from the common, and minded his pigs and his cow, and put by odd shillings for occasional need. Notice that putting-by of shillings. It was not the whole, it was only the completion, of the peasant's thrift. At a pinch he could even do without the money, paying for what he wanted with a sack of potatoes, or a day's work with his donkey-cart; but a little money put by was a convenience. When it was wanted, it was wanted in lump sums—ten shillings now, say, for a little pig; and then fifteen shillings or so in six weeks' time for mending the donkey-cart, and so on; and, thanks to the real savings in the shape of food and firing ready for use, the shillings, however come by, could be hoarded up.

But under the new thrift they cannot be so hoarded up; nor, fortunately, are the little lump sums so necessary as before. The real savings now, the real stores of useful capital, are no longer in the cottager's home. They are in shops. What the modern labourer chiefly requires, therefore, is not a little hoard of money lying by, but a regular supply of money, a constant stream of it, flowing in, to enable him to go to the shops regularly. In a word, he wants an income—a steady income of shillings. And since his earnings are not steady—since his income may cease any day, and continue in abeyance for weeks at a time, during which the shops will be closed against him, his chief economy is directed upon the object of insuring his weekly income. Most miserably for him, he has never been able to insure it against all reverses. Against trade depression, which throws him out of work and dries up the stream of money that should come flowing in, he has no protection. He has none if his employer should go bankrupt, or leave the neighbourhood, and dismiss him; none against the competition of machinery. Still, the labourers do as much as they can.

Sickness, at least, does not find them unprepared. To cover loss of wages during sickness, they pay into a benefit society. The more careful, indeed, pay into two—the Oddfellows or the Foresters, or some such society—and a local " slate-club." I have known men out of work living on tea and bread, and not much of that, so that they may keep up their club payments, and be sure of an income if they should fall sick; and I have known men so circumstanced immediately feel the advantage if sickness should actually fall upon them.

This is the new thrift, which has replaced that of the peasant. I do not say that there is no other saving—that no little sums are hoarded up; for, in fact, I could name one or two men who, after illness protracted to the stage when sick-pay from the club is reduced, have still fought off destitution with the small savings from better times. In most cases, however, no hoarding is possible. The club takes all the spare money; and the club alone stands between the labourer and destitution. And let this be clearly understood. At first it looks as if the member of a club had money invested in his society—money there, instead of perishable goods at home. Yet, in fact, that is not the case. His payments into the club funds are no investment. They bring him no profit; they are not a useful capital that can be renewed with interest. At the Christmas " share-out " he does get back a part of the twenty-six shillings contributed to the slate-club during the year; but the two pounds a year paid to the benefit society are his no longer; they cannot be " realized "; they are gone beyond reclaiming. Though he be out of work and his family starving, he cannot touch the money; to derive any advantage from it he himself must first fall ill. That is what the modern thrift means to the labourer. It does nothing to further—on the contrary, it retards—his prosperity; but it helps him in a particular kind of adversity. It drains his personal wealth away, and leaves him destitute of his capital; it robs his wife and children of his savings; but in return it makes him one of a brotherhood which guarantees to him a minimum income for a short time, if he should be out of health.

An oldish man, who had been telling me one evening how they used to live in his boyhood, looked pensively across the valley when he had done, and so stood for a minute or two, as if trying to recover his impressions of that lost time. At last, with appearance of an effort to speak patiently, " Ah," he said, " they tells me times are better now, but I can't see it;" and it was plain enough that he thought our present times the worse. So far as this valley is concerned I incline to agree with him, although in general it is a debatable question. On the one hand, it may be that the things a labourer can buy at a shop for fifteen shillings a week are more in quantity and variety, if not better in quality, than those which his forefathers could produce by their own industry; and to that extent the advantage is with the present times. But, on the other hand, the fifteen shillings are not every week forthcoming; and whereas the old-time cottager out of work could generally find something profitable to do for himself, the modern man, having once got his garden into order, stands unprofitably idle.

Perhaps the worst is that, owing to the lowness of their wages, the people have never been able to give the new thrift a fair trial. After all, they miss the lump sums laid by against need. If their earnings would ever overtake their expenses and give a little margin, they might do better; but buying, as they are obliged to do, from hand to mouth, they buy at extravagant prices. Coal, for instance, which costs me about twenty-six shillings for a ton, costs the labourer half as much again as that, because he can only pay for a hundredweight or so at a time. So, too, the boots he can get for four or five shillings a pair are the dearest of all boots. They wear out in a couple of months or so, and another pair must be bought almost before another four or five shillings can be spared. In its smaller degree, a still more absurd difficulty handicaps the people in dealing with their own fruit-crops. To make raspberry or gooseberry jam should be, you would think, an economy delightful to the cottage women, if only as a piece of old-fashioned thrift; yet they rarely do it. If they had the necessary utensils, still the weekly money at their disposal will not run to the purchase of extra firing and sugar. It is all too little for every-day purposes, and they are glad to eke it out by selling their fruit for middle-class women to preserve, though in the end they have to buy for their own families an inferior quality of jam at a far higher price.

Wherever you follow it up, you will find the modern thrift not quite successful in the cottages. It is not elastic enough; or, rather, the people's means are not elastic enough, and will not stretch to its demands. There is well-being in it—variety of food, for instance, and comfort of clothing—as soon as both ends can be made to meet and to lap over a little; but it strains the small incomes continually to the breaking-point, so that every other consideration has to give way under it to a pitiful calculation of pence. For the sake of pence the people who keep fowls sell the eggs, and feed their children on bread and margarine; and, on the same principle, they do not even seek to produce other things which are well within their power to produce, but are too luxurious for their means. " 'Twouldn't be no use for me to grow strawberries," a man explained; " my children'd have 'em." It sounded a strange reason, for to what better use could strawberries be put? But it shows how tightly the people are bound down by their commercial conditions. In order to make the Saturday's shopping easier, they must weigh the shillings and pence value of everything they possess and everything they attempt to do.

These considerations, however, though showing that present times are not good, do not prove that they are worse than past times. It may be that there was poverty in the valley before the enclosure of the common quite as severe as there is now;

and, so far as concerns mere economics, that event did but
change the mode of the struggle for existence, without greatly
affecting its intensity. People are poor in a different way now,
that is all. Hence, in its more direct results, the loss of the
common has not mattered much, and it might be forgotten if
those results were the only ones.

But they are not the only ones. The results have spread
from the economic centre outwards until the whole life of the
people has been affected, new influences coming into play
which previously were but little felt. So searching, indeed, has
the change been, and so revolutionary, that anything like a full
account of it would be out of the question. The chapters that
follow, therefore, do not pretend to deal with it at all exhaus-
tively; at most they will but draw attention to a few of its more
striking aspects.

X

COMPETITION

WHEN the half-peasant men of the valley began to enter the
labour market as avowed wage-earners, a set of conditions confronted them which we are apt to think of as established by a
law of Nature, but which, in fact, may be almost unknown in
a peasant community. For the first time the importance of a
" demand for labour " came home to them. I do not say that
it was wholly a new thing; but to the older villagers it had, not
been, as it is now to their descendants, the dominating factor in
their struggle for life. On the contrary, in proportion as their
labour was bestowed immediately on productive work for their
own uses, the question whether there was a demand for labour
elsewhere did not arise. The common was indifferent; it

wanted none of them. It neither asked them to avail themselves of its resources, nor paid them money for doing so, nor refused employment to one because another was already engaged there. But to-day, instead of going for a livelihood to the impartial heath, the people must wait for others to set them to work. The demand which they supply is their own no longer, and no longer, therefore, is their living in their own hands. Of all the old families in the village, I think there are only two left now who have not drifted wholly into this dependent state; but I know numbers of labourers, often out of work, whose grandfathers were half independent of employers.

In theory, no doubt the advantage ought to be with the present times. Under the new system a far larger population is able to live in the parish than could possibly have been supported here under the old; for now, in place of the scanty products of the little valley and the heaths, the stores of the whole world may be drawn upon by the inhabitants in return for the wages they earn. Only there is the awkward condition that they must earn wages. Those limitless stores cannot be approached by the labourer until he is invited—until there is " a demand " for his labour. Property owners, or capitalists, standing between him and the world's capital, are able to pick and choose between him and his neighbours as the common never did, and to decide which of them shall work and have some of the supplies.

And as a consequence of this picking and choosing, competition amongst the labourers seeking to be employed has become the accepted condition of getting a living in the village, and it is to a great extent a new condition. Previously there was little room for anything of the kind. The old thrift lent itself to co-operation rather. I admit that I have never heard of any system being brought into the activities of this valley, such as I witnessed lately in another part of England, where the small farmers, supplying an external market, and having no hired labour, were helping one another to get their corn harvested, all being solicitous for their neighbours' welfare, and giving, not selling, their labour. Here the conditions hardly required such wholesale co-operation as that; but in lesser matters both kindliness and economy would counsel the people to be mutually helpful, and there is no reason to doubt that the counsel was taken. Those who had donkey-carts would willingly bring home turfs for those who had none, in return for help with their own turf-cutting. The bread-ovens, I know, were at the disposal of others besides the owners. At pig-killing, at thatching, at clearing out wells (where, in fact, I have seen the thing going on), the people would put themselves at one another's service. They still do so in cases where there is no question of earning money for a living. And if the spirit of friendly co-operation is alive now, when it can so rarely be put in practice, one may readily suppose that it was fairly vigorous fifty years ago.

But no spirit of co-operation may now prompt one wage-earner to ask, or another to proffer, assistance in working for wages. As well might one shopkeeper propose to wait on another's customers for him. Employers would not have it; still less would those who are employed. A man may be fainting at his job, but none dare help him. He would resent, he would fear, the proposal. The job is, as it were, his property; as long as he can stand and see he must hold it against all comers, because in losing hold he loses his claim upon the world's supplies of the necessaries of life.

In spite of all the latent good-will, therefore, and in spite of the fact that the cottagers are all on the same social level, intimacies do not thrive amongst them. If there was formerly any parochial sentiment in the village, any sense of community of interest, it has all been broken up by the exigencies of competitive wage-earning, and each family stands by itself, aloof from all the others. The interests clash. Men who might be helpful friends in other circumstances are in the position of rival tradesmen competing for the patronage of customers.

Not now may their labour be a bond of friendship between them; it is a commodity with a market value, to be sold in the market. Hence, just as in trade, every man for himself is the rule with the villagers; just as in trade, the misfortune of one is the opportunity of another. All the maxims of competitive commerce apply fully to the vendor of his own labour. There must be " no friendship in business "; the weakest must go to the wall. Each man is an individualist fighting for his own hand; and to give as little as he can for as much as he can get is good policy for him, with precisely the same limitations as those that govern the trading of the retail merchant, tormented with the conflicting necessities of overcharging and under-selling.

It follows that the villagers are a prey to jealousy and sus-picion—not, perhaps, when they meet at the public-house or on the road, but in the presence of employers, when any question of employment arises. At such times one would think that labouring men have no critics so unkindly as their own neigh-bours and equals. It is true those who are in constant work are commended; but if you ask about a man who is " on the market " and open for any work that may be going, his rivals are unlikely to answer generously. " So-and-So? . . . H'm! . . . He do's his best; but he don't seem to get *through*, some-how." " Old Who-is-it? Asked *he* to come and help me, have ye? Well, you'll judge for yourself; but I don't hardly fancy he'll suit." Or, again: " Well, we all knows how 'tis with What's-his-name. I don't say but what he keeps on work right enough; but he'll have to jump about smarter 'n what I've ever knowed 'n, if he's to work 'long o' me." So, too, often, and sometimes in crueller terms, I have heard efficient labourers speak of their neighbours. Certainly it is not all envy. An active man finds it penance to work with a slow one, and worse than penance; for his own reputation may suffer, if his own output of work should be diminished by the other's fault. That neighbour of mine engaged at hop-drying doubtless had good grounds for exasperation with the helper sent into the kiln, when he complained to the master: " Call that a *man* you sent me? If that's what you calls a man, I'd sooner you let me send for my old woman! Blamed if she wouldn't do better than that feller!" Detraction like this, no doubt, is often justified; but when it becomes the rule, the only possible inference is that an instinctive jealousy prompts men to it, in instinctive self-preservation.

Yet there are depths of dishonour—depths not unknown amongst employers—into which the village labourers will rarely condescend to plunge, acute though the temptation may be. Not once have I met with an instance of one man deliberately scheming to get another man's job away from him. A labourer unable to keep up with his work will do almost anything to avoid having a helper thrust upon him—he fears the introduction of a possible rival into his preserve. But this is not the same thing as pushing another man out; it has no resemblance to the behaviour of the hustling capitalist, who opens his big business with the definite intention of capturing trade away from little businesses. That is a course to which my impoverished neighbours will not stoop. The nearest thing to it which I have known was the case of those men mentioned in an earlier chapter, who applied for Bettesworth's work during his last illness. They came, however, believing the place to be vacant; and one and all, with a sincerity I never doubted, deprecated the idea of desiring to take it away from him. In fact, the application was distasteful to them. Nothing, I believe, would have prevailed upon them to make it, short of that hunger for constant employment which many of the men feel now, under their new competitive thrift. That they should have been scrupulous at all was to their credit. All their circumstances constrain the people to be selfish, secret about their hopes, swift to be first in the field where a chance occurs. And it is surprising how vigilant a lookout is kept, and how wide a district it covers. By what routes the news of new employment travels I do not know, but travel it does, fast and far. Men rise early and walk many miles to be before others at some place where they have heard of work to be had; and one gets the impression, sometimes, of a population silently but keenly watching to see what opportunity of well-being may suddenly fall to them, not in general, but individually.

Do what they will to be neighbourly, competition for the privilege of earning wages separates them sooner or later. There were two men I knew who maintained a sort of comradeship in work during several years, so that one of them would not take a job unless there was room for the other, and if either was paid off, the other left with him. They were amongst the ablest labourers in the parish, used to working long hours at high pressure, and indifferent to what they did, provided that the pay was good. I heard of them from time to time—now at railway work, now at harvesting, now helping where a bridge was being built, and so on. It was the depression of the winter of 1908-09 that finally broke up their comradeship. During those miserable months even these two were unemployed, and went short of food at times; and now they are working separately—competing one against the other, in fact.

XI

HUMILIATION

STILL more than the relations of the villagers with their own kind their relations with other sorts of people have suffered change under the new thrift. To just that extent to which the early inhabitants of the valley were peasants, they formed, as it were, a separate group, careless of the outer world and its concerns. They could afford to ignore it, and to be ignored by it.

To them, so well suited with their own outlook and customs, it was a matter of small importance, though all England should have other views than theirs, and other manners. And the outer world, on its side, was equally indifferent. It left the villagers to go their own queer way, and recognized—as it does in the case of other separate groups of folk, such as fishermen or costermongers—that what seemed singular in them was probably justified by the singularity of their circumstances. Nobody supposed that they were a wrong or a regrettable type who ought to be " done good to " or reformed. They belonged to their own set. They were English, of course; but they were outside the ordinary classifications of English society.

Even towards those of them who went out of the valley to earn wages this was still the attitude. They went out as peasants, and were esteemed because they had the ability of peasants. In much the same way as country folk on the Continent take their country produce into town markets the men of this valley took, into the hop-grounds and fields of the neighbouring valley, or into its old-fashioned streets and stable yards, their toughness, their handiness, their intimate understanding of country crafts; and, returning home in the evening, they slipped back again into their natural peasant state, without any feeling of disharmony from the day's employment.

There was no reason why it should be otherwise. Although, at work, they had come into contact with people unlike themselves in some ways, the contrast was not of such a kind that it disheartened or seemed to disgrace them. At the time of the enclosure of the common, a notable development, certainly, was beginning amongst the employing classes, but it had not then proceeded far. Of course the day of the yeoman farmer was almost done; and with it there had disappeared some of that equality which permitted wage-earning men to be on such easy terms with their masters as one hears old people describe. No longer, probably, would a farmer take a nickname from his men, or suffer them to call his daughters familiarly by their

Christian names; and no longer did master and man live on quite the same quality of food, or dress in the same sort of clothes. Nevertheless the distinction between employers and employed—between the lower middle-class and the working-class—was not nearly so marked fifty years ago as it has since become. The farmers, for their part, were still veritable country folk, inheritors themselves of a set of rural traditions nearly akin to those of the peasant squatters in this valley. And even the townsmen, who were the only others who could give employment to these villagers, were extremely countrified in character. In their little sleepy old town—not half its present size, and the centre then of an agricultural and especially a hop-growing district—people were intimately interested in country things. No matter what a man's trade or profession—linen-draper, or saddler, or baker, or lawyer, or banker—he found it worth while to watch the harvests, and to know a great deal about cattle and sheep, and more than a great deal about hops. Some of the tradesmen were, in fact, growing wealthy as hop-planters; and one and all identified themselves with the outdoor industries of the neighbourhood. And though some grew rich, and changed their style of living, they did not change their mental equipment, but continued (as I myself remember) more " provincial " than many a farmer is nowadays. All their thoughts, all their ideas, could be quite well expressed in the West Surrey and Hampshire dialect, which the townspeople, like the village folk, continued to speak.

Meanwhile, the work required by these employers ran, as yet, very much on antiquated lines. Perhaps it was that the use of machinery had received a set-back, twenty years earlier, by the " Swing Riots," of which a few memories still survive; at any rate haymaking, harvesting, threshing—all the old tasks, indeed—were still done by hand; thatch had not gone out of use for barns and stables; nor, for house-roofs had imported slates quite taken the place of locally made tiles. The truth is, the town, in its more complex way, had not itself passed far beyond the primitive stage of dependence on local resources and local skill. It is really surprising how few were the materials, or even the finished goods, imported into it at that time. Clothing stuffs and metals were the chief of them. Of course the grocers (not " provision merchants " then) did their small trade in sugar and coffee, and tea and spices; there was a tinware shop, an ironmonger's, a wine-merchant's; and all these necessarily were supplied from outside. But, on the other hand, no foreign meat or flour, or hay or straw or timber, found their way into the town, and comparatively few manufactured products from other parts of England. Carpenters still used the oak and ash and elm of the neighbourhood, sawn out for them by local sawyers : the wheelwright, because iron was costly, mounted his cartwheels on huge axles fashioned by himself out of the hardest beech; the smith, shoeing horses or putting tyres on wheels, first made the necessary nails for himself, hammering them out on his own anvil. So, too, with many other things. Boots, brushes, earthenware, butter and lard, candles, bricks—they were all of local make; cheese was brought back from Weyhill Fair in the waggons which had carried down the hops; in short, to an extent hard to realize, the town was independent of commerce as we know it now, and looked to the farms and forests and the claypits and coppices of the neighbourhood for its supplies. A leisurely yet steady traffic in rural produce therefore passed along its streets, because it was the life-centre, the heart, of its own countryside; and the village labourer, going in and out upon his town tasks, or even working all day in some secluded yard behind the street, still found a sort of homeliness in the materials he handled, and was in touch with the ideas and purposes of his employer.

Owing to these same circumstances, the wage-earners of that day enjoyed what their descendants would consider a most blissful freedom from anxiety. On the one side, the demand for labour was fairly steady. It was the demand of a community not rapidly growing in numbers, nor yet subject to crazes and sudden changes of a fashion—a community patiently, nay, cheerfully, conservative in its ambitions, not given to rash speculation, but contented to go on plodding on in its time-honoured and modest well-being. What the towns-folk wanted one year they wanted the next, and so onwards with but quiet progress. And as the demand for labour was thus steady, so on the other side was the supply of it. A dis-satisfied employer could not advertise, then, in a London daily paper, and get scores of men applying to him for work at a day's notice; nor, indeed, would strangers have been able to do the work in many cases, so curiously was its character deter-mined by local conditions. Besides, town opinion, still preju-diced by memories of the old Poor Law, would have viewed with extreme disfavour, had such an experiment ever been tried, the importation of men and families whose coming must surely result in pauperism for somebody, and in a consequent charge upon the rates.

So, putting together the leading factors—namely, a steady demand for countrified labour, a steady supply of it, and an employing class full of country ideas—we get a rough idea of the conditions of wage-earning in the neighbourhood, when the folk of this valley, fenced out from their common, were forced to look to wage-earning as their sole means of living. That the conditions were ideal it would be foolish to suppose; but that, for villagers at least, they had certain advantages over present conditions is not to be denied. Especially we may note two unpleasing features of modern wage-earning which had not then made their appearance.

In the first place, the work itself was interesting to do, was almost worth doing for its own sake, when it still called for much old-world skill and knowledge, and when the praises of the master were the praises of an expert who well knew what he was talking about. On these terms, it was no mean pleasure that the able labouring men had in their labour. They took a pride in it—as you may soon discern if you will listen to the older men talking. I have heard them boast, as of a triumph, of the fine flattering surprise of some master, when he had come to look at their day's work, and found it more forward, or better done, than he had dared to hope. The words he said are treasured up with delight, and repeated with enthusiasm, after many years.

As for the other point, it has already been touched upon. Harsh the employers might be—more callous by far, I believe, than they are now; but in their general outlook they were not, as yet, so very far removed from the men who worked for them. Their ideas of good and bad were such as the peasant labourer from this valley could understand; and master and man were not greatly out of touch in the matter of civilization. It made a vast difference to the labourer's comfort. He might be hectored, bullied, cheated even, but he hardly felt himself degraded too. It was not a being out of another sphere that oppressed him; not one who despised him, not one whose motives were strange and mysterious. The cruellest oppression was inhuman rather than unhuman—the act, after all, only of a more powerful, not of a more dazzling, personage—so that it produced in him no humiliating sense of belonging to an inferior order of creation. And, of course, oppression was exceptional. Employers were obliged to get on comfortably with their workpeople, by the conditions governing the supply of labour. I have in my mind several cases mentioned to me by people long ago dead, in which men for various faults (drunkenness in one instance, theft in another) were dismissed from their employment again and again, yet as often reinstated, because the master found it easier to put up with their faults than to do without their skill. It may be inferred, therefore, that ordinary men got along fairly well with their masters in the ordinary course.

This state of things, however, has gradually passed away.

As I shall show in another chapter, the labourer may now take but little interest and but little pride in his work; but the change in that direction is not more pronounced than is the change in the relations between the villagers and the employing classes. It is a cruel evil that the folk of the valley have suffered there. No longer are they a group whose peculiarities are respected while their qualities are esteemed. In their intercourse with the outer world they have become, as it were, degraded, humiliated; and when they go out of the valley to earn wages, it is to take the position of an inferior and almost servile race. The reason is that the employing class, as a whole, has moved on, leaving the labourers where they were, until now a great gulf divides them. Merely in relative wealth, if that were all, the difference has widened enormously. Seventy or eighty years ago, I have heard say, the shopkeeper in the town who had as much as a hundred pounds put by was thought a rich man. There are now many artisans there whose savings exceed that figure, while the property of the townsmen who employ labour is, of course, valued often in thousands. The labouring people alone remain without savings, as poor as their grandfathers when the common was first enclosed.

But it is a question of civilization far more than of wealth that now divides the employing classes from the employed. The former have discarded much of their provincialism; they are astir with ambitions and ideas at which the old town would have stood aghast. In beliefs and in tastes they are a new people. They have new kinds of knowledge; almost one may say that they use their brains in new ways; and the result is that between them and the village labourer mutual understanding has broken down. How far the separation has gone is betrayed in the fact that the countrified speech, common to village and town fifty years ago, has become a subject of derision to the town-people, forgetful of their own ancestry. So, in field and street and shop, the two kinds of folk meet face to face, not with an outlook, and hardly with a speech, which both can appreciate, but like distinct races, the one dominant, the other subject.

And, all but inevitably, the breach is daily widened by the conditions on which the new civilization of the employing class is based. For, with all its good features, it is rather a barbaric civilization, in this sense—that it is more a matter of fineness in possessions than in personal qualities. It cannot be maintained without a costly apparatus of dress and furniture, and of drudges to do the dirty work; and consequently it demands success in that competitive thrift which gives a good money-income. Without that the employers are nowhere. They are themselves driven very hard; they must make things pay; to secure the means of civilization for themselves, they must get them out of the labourer with his eighteen shillings a week. In vain, therefore, are they persuaded by their newest ideas to see in him an Englishman as good as themselves : they may assent to the principle, but in practice it is as imperative as ever to make him a profitable drudge. Accordingly, those relations of mutual approval which were not uncommon of old between master and man cannot now be maintained. If it is impossible for the village folk to understand the town folk, it is equally impossible for the town folk to understand the village folk. They cannot afford to understand. The peasant outlook is out of date—a cast-off thing; and for cleaving to it the labourer is despised. If he could be civilized, and yet be made to "pay," that is what would best suit the middle-classes; and that is really the impossible object at which they aim, when they try to "do him good." They want to make him more like themselves, and yet keep him in his place of dependence and humiliation.

It must be said that amongst a section of the employers there is no desire to "do good" even on these terms. While the labouring people, on their side, betray little or no class feeling of hostility towards employers, the converse is not true, but jealousy, suspicion, some fear—the elements of bitter class-war, in fact—frequently mark the attitude of middle-class people towards the labouring class. It seems to be forgotten that the men are English. One hears them spoken of as an alien and objectionable race, worth nothing but to be made to work. The unemployment which began to beggar so many of my village neighbours after the South African War was actually welcomed by numerous employers in this district. " It will do the men good," people said to me; " it will teach them their place. They were getting too independent." The election of 1906, when the Conservative member for the division was unseated, brought out a large crop of similarly malevolent expressions. " Look at the class of people who have the vote," said a disgusted villa lady, with her nose in the air. " Only the low, ignorant people wear those colours," another lady assured her little boy, whose eyes preferred " those colours " to the favours in his own buttonhole. More pointed was the overheard remark of a well-to-do employer, irritated by the election crowds in the town : " As my wife says, it was bad enough before. The children of the lower classes used, as it was, to take the inside of the pavement, and we had to walk on the kerb. But now we shall be driven out into the road."

I would not mention these things were it not for their significance to the village folk. By becoming wage-earners solely, the villagers have fallen into the disfavour of an influential section of the middle-classes, most of whom have no other desire than to keep them in a sufficient state of servility to be useful. How else is one to interpret that frequent middle-class outcry against education : " What are we going to do for servants ? " or how else the grudging attitude taken up towards the few comforts that cottage people are able to enjoy ? I listened lately to two men talking of " Tariff Reform "—one of them a commercial traveller, lofty in his patriotism. When mention was made of some old man's tale, that in his boyhood he rarely tasted meat, " unless a sheep died," the commercial traveller commented scornfully, "And now every working man in the kingdom thinks he must have meat twice a day "— as though such things ought not to be in the British Empire. The falsehood of the remark enhanced its significance. It was the sort of thing to say in hotel-bars, or in the offices of commerce—the sort of thing that goes down well with employers. It indicated that the animus of which I am speaking is almost a commonplace. In truth, I have heard it expressed dozens of times, in dozens of ways, yet always with the same implied suggestion, that the English labouring classes are a lower order of beings, who must be treated accordingly.

And yet employers of this type, representing the wealth, perhaps, but by no means the culture, of modern civilization, are, in fact, nearer to the unlettered labourers in their outlook, and are therefore by far less embarrassing to them, than those of another and kindlier type which figures largely in this parish to-day. Those people for whom the enclosure of the common, as it has turned out, made room in the valley—I mean the well-to-do residents—employ local labour, not for profit at all, but to minister to their own pleasure, in their gardens and stables, and the majority of them would be genuinely glad to be helpful to their poorer neighbours. The presence of poverty reproaches them; their consciences are uneasy; or, better still, some kind of regard, some kind of respect, goes out from them towards the toilsome men and the overburdened women whom, in fact, they have displaced. Yet compassion is not the same thing as understanding, and the cottagers know very well that even their best friends of this kind have neither the knowledge nor the taste to appreciate them in their own way. Sympathy for their troubles—yes, there is that; but sympathy with their enjoyments hardly any property-owner dreams of cultivating; and this is the more true the more the property-owner has been polished by his own civilization. A lady long resident here was quite surprised to hear from me, some months ago, that the cottagers are ardent gardeners. "Dear me!" she said; "I had no idea of it." And yet one of the ablest men of the parish had tended her own garden for years.

Hence it is in their intercourse with these—the well-meaning and cultivated—that the villagers are most at a loss. In those embittered employers who merely seek to make money out of him the labourer does at least meet with some keen recognition of his usefulness; but with these others he is all at sea. Non-introspective, a connoisseur of garden crops and of pigstyes, and of saved-up seeds; cunning to understand the "set" of spade or hoe, and the temper of scythe and fag-hook; jealous of the encroachment of gravelled walk or evergreen hedge upon the useful soil; an expert in digging and dunging—he is very well aware that the praises of the villa-people employing him are ignorant praises. His best skill is, after all, overlooked. The cunning of his craft excites in them none of the sympathy of a fellow-expert, and is but poorly rewarded by their undiscriminating approval. At the same time, the things which these people require of him—the wanton things they ask him to do with the soil, levelling it to make lawns, wasting it upon shrubberies and drives, while they fence-in the heath patches and fence-out the public—prove to him more fully than any language can do that they put a different sort of value upon the countryside from its old value, and that they care not a straw for the mode of life that was his before they came here. All their ways are eloquent condemnation of his tastes. And yet again, while his old skill fails to be understood, and his old outlook to be appreciated, he finds that the behaviour preferred in him is oftener than not a behaviour which his forefathers would have thought silly, to say the least—a finikin, fastidious behaviour, such as he would scorn to practise at home. Thus in all ways the employers most conscientiously humane are those who can least avoid, in their tastes and their whole manner of living, snubbing him and setting him down in an inferior place. They cannot help it, now that they have thrust themselves upon him as neighbours. The more they interest themselves in him, the more glaringly is the difference which separates themselves from him brought out.

Whether, if the common had remained open, the villagers could still have held aloof, at this time of day, from the movements of the outer world is a question not worth discussion. The enclosure was brought to pass; the keystone was knocked out of the arch; and here are some of the indirect consequences. From a position in which the world's distinctions of class and caste were hardly noticed—a position which was, so to speak, an island of refuge, where self-respect could be preserved in preserving the old rough peasant ways—the valley folk have been forced into such relations with the world outside the valley as we have seen. They are no longer a separate set, unclassified, but a grade has been assigned to them in the classification of society at large, and it is wellnigh the lowest grade of all, for only the pauper and criminal classes are below them. In this sense, therefore, they are a " degraded " people, though by no fault of their own. Amongst " the masses " is where they are counted. Moreover, since they are now, as we have seen, competing against one another for the right to live, none of the concessions are made to them now that were of old made to the group of them, but they count, and are judged, individually, amongst the millions of the English proletariat. " Inferiority " has come into their lives; it is expected of them to treat almost everybody else as a superior person. But the cruellest indignity of all is that, although we regard them as inferiors, we still look to them to admire and live up to our standards; and they are to conform to our civilization, yet without the income it requires or the social recognition it should secure. And if they will not do this willingly, then shall they be coerced, or at least kept in order by " temperance " and other " reforming " legislation, and by the police.

XII

THE HUMILIATED

THE effects of this " inferiority " which has been thrust upon
the villagers are not exactly conspicuous in any particular
direction. As it has been shown already, the people themselves
seem almost unaware of any grievance in the matter, the
change having come upon them too gradually for it to be
sharply felt. They bear no malice against their employers.
You would hardly learn, from anything that they consciously
say or do, that in becoming so humiliated they have been hurt
in their feelings, or have found it necessary to change their
habits.

Indeed, the positive alteration in their manners, by which I
mean the adoption of new ways in place of old ones, has probably not amounted to a great deal. I admit that I have no
means of estimating how much it does amount to. During
fifty years, in which every cottager must now and then have
become aware of constraint put upon him or her by the superior
attitude of the employing class, it is quite possible that there
have been innumerable small concessions and adaptations of
manner, and that these have accumulated into a general change
which would surprise us if it could be measured. But I incline
to think that the effects of class-pressure have been chiefly
negative; that, while employers have been adopting new modes
of life, all that has happened to the labouring folk here in the
valley is that this or that habit, found inexpedient at last, has
been quietly dropped. A sort of reserve in the village temper,
a want of gaiety, a subdued air—this, which one cannot help
observing, is probably the shadow cast upon the people from
the upraised middle-class. It looks suggestive, too. Yet, upon
examining it, one fails to find in it any definite token that
would show exactly how and where the village temper has

been touched, or in what light " superior " persons are regarded in the cottages. The people appear enigmatic. They keep their own counsel. Whether they are bewildered or amused at the behaviour of employers, or alarmed or embittered by it, or actually indifferent to it, no sign escapes them when members of the employing class are by.

In these circumstances, it is instructive to turn aside for a while from the grown-up people of the village, and to consider their children; because the children do not learn about the employing class by direct intercourse, but derive from their parents such ideas as they have of what is safe to do, and what is proper, where employing people are concerned. As soon as this truth is realized, a curious significance appears in some characteristic habits of the village school boys and girls. The boys, especially, deserve remark. That they are in general " rough," " uncivilized," I suppose might go without saying. It might also go without saying, were it not that the comparison turns out to be useful, that in animal spirits, physical courage, love of mischief and noise, they are at least a match for middle-class boys who go to the town grammar-school. I wish I could say that they have an equally good sense of " playing the game," an equally strong *esprit de corps*, and so on. Unfortunately, these traditions have hardly reached the village school as yet, and perhaps will not easily make their way there, amongst the children of parents whom the struggle for life compels to be so suspicious and jealous. The question is, however, beside the point now. Viewed without prejudice, the village boys must be thought quite as good material as any other English boys; you can see that there is the making of strong and brave men in them. With similar chances they would not be inferior in any respect to the sons of the middle classes.

But under existing conditions the two sorts of boys develop some curious differences of habit. Where those from middle-class homes are self-possessed, those from the labourers' cot-

E

tages are not merely shy, not merely uncouth and lubberly; they grow furtive, suspicious, timid as wild animals, on the watch for a chance to run. Audacious enough at bird's-nesting, sliding, tree-climbing, fighting, and impertinent enough towards people of their own kind, they quail before the first challenge of " superiority." All aplomb goes from them then. It is distressing to see how they look : with an expression of whimpering rebellion, as though the superior person had unhuman qualities, not .to be reckoned on—as though there were danger in his presence. An incident of a few years ago, very trumpery in itself, displayed to me in the sharpest distinctness the contrast between the two orders of boys in this respect. In the hedge which parts my garden from the lane there is a nut-tree, too tempting to all boys when the nuts are ripe. At that season one hears whispered and ex-clamatory confabulations going on in the lane, and then large stones go crashing up into the tree, falling back sometimes within the hedge, where there is a bit of grass and a garden seat. Occasionally, playing the absurd part of irate property-owner, I have gone to the gate near by to drive off the offenders, but have opened it only in time to see a troop of urchins, alarmed by the click of the gate-latch, scurrying away like rabbits round the bend of the lane. One Sunday afternoon, however, when I looked out after a stone had fallen nearly on my head, it was to find two boys calmly waiting for me to approach them. Their school caps showed them to be two boys of the grammar-school. The interview went comically. Upon being told crossly that they were a nuisance, the boys apologized—an act which seemed to put me in the wrong. In my annoyance at that, I hinted ironically that, in fact, I was a benevolent person, quite willing to admit boys inside the hedge to pick up nuts, if nuts they really must have. Then I turned away. To my astonishment, they took me at my word, fol-lowed me into the garden, and calmly began to pick up nuts; while I withdrew, discomfited. I have since smiled to think of the affair; but I recall it now with more interest, for the sake of the contrast it affords between middle-class boys and labouring-class boys in exactly similar circumstances. Where the former behave confidently, because they feel safe, the latter are overtaken by panic, and run to cover.

In this light another curious fact about the village boys gains in significance, supposing it to be indeed a fact. From the nature of the case, proof is not possible, but I have a strong impression that, excepting to go to the town, the boys of the village rarely, if ever, stray into neighbouring parishes, or more than a few hundred yards away from their parents' homes. One exception must be noted. In the lonely and silent fir-woods, which begin in the next valley and stretch away over ridge and dell for some miles from south-east to south-west, one sometimes comes upon a group of village children—little boys and girls together—filling sacks with fir-cones, and pushing an old perambulator to carry the load. But these are hardly voluntary expeditions; and the boys are always very small ones, while the girls are in charge. The bigger boys, of from ten to thirteen years old, do not go into the woods. They play in the roads and pathways, or on the corners of unused land, and as a rule within sight or call of home. I have never seen any of them, as I have occasionally seen middle-class boys from the town, rambling far afield in the outlying country, and my belief is that they would be considerably scared to find themselves in such unfamiliar scenes.

Assuming that I am right, yet another contrast presents itself. It was in this very neighbourhood that William Cobbett, as a little boy, played off upon the huntsman that trick of revenge which he bragged about in after-life. For five or six miles across country, over various streams, through woods and heaths and ploughed upland fields, he made his way all alone, dragging his red herring, perfectly confident in himself, never at a loss to know where he was, but thoroughly familiar with the lie of the land most suitable for his game. Of course, not many boys are Cobbetts. Yet many of the village boys, even now, would be his match at other games. For here, on the shelving sand-banks beside the stream, I have seen them enjoying rough-and-tumble romps like those which the little Cobbett lived to think the best part of his education; and they do it with a recklessness which even he can scarce have surpassed. But in getting about the country they do not so much as begin to emulate him. Of course, it is true that now they have to spend their days in school; true, too, that the enclosures of land throughout the neighbourhood have made wandering less easy in our times; nevertheless, within a few miles there are woods and heath-lands in plenty for adventurous boys, as those of the middle-class are aware; yet those of the village never risk the adventure. I can but infer that they are afraid of something, and a moment's thought discloses what they fear. Just as in meddling with my nut-tree, so everywhere they are in danger of trouble with people of the propertied or employing kind; and behind these people stands the policeman, and behind the policeman that dim object of dread called " a summons." This it is that keeps the village children within the bounds familiar to them, where they know who is who, and what property belongs to which owner, and how far they may risk doing mischief, and round what corners they may scamper into safety.

The caution they display is not unnecessary. Somehow, middle-class boys do not get into trouble with the law; but it happens not infrequently that a few little villagers are " pulled up " before a magistrate for trivial acts of mischief, and if the worst punishment inflicted upon them is a shilling fine and costs, which their parents pay, that is enough to make "a summons " a very dreadful thing to a little boy. Out of eighteen shillings a week, his father cannot afford " a shilling and costs " for a piece of mischief, as the little boy is but too likely to be shown.

Children's memories are short, however, and it takes more

than an occasional punishment of two or three to inspire in
them all a timorousness so instinctive in character as that of
these village boys. At the back of it there must be a more
constant and pervasive influence. And, to come to the point at
last, I think that the boys are swayed, unwittingly, by an attitude in the grown-up people with whom they live—an attitude
of habitual wariness, not to say fear, in regard to everything
connected with property and employers. This is what makes
the timidity of the village urchins interesting. We may discern
in it the expression of a feeling prevalent throughout the cottages—an unreasoned but convinced distrust of propertied folk,
and a sense of being unprotected and helpless against their
privileges and power. Here, accordingly, is one direction in
which class distinction has seriously affected the villagers. It
would be an exaggeration to say that they feel like outlaws; but
they are vaguely aware of constraint imposed upon them by
laws and prejudices which are none too friendly to people of
their kind. One divines it in their treatment of the village
policeman. There is probably no lonelier man in the parish
than the constable. Of course he meets with civility, but his
company is avoided. One hears him mentioned in those same
accents of grudging caution which the villagers use in speaking
of unfriendly property-owners, as though he belonged to that
alien caste. The cottagers feel that they themselves are the
people whom he is stationed in the valley to watch.

They feel it; nor can it be denied that there is some excuse
for the feeling. It is true that they far outnumber the employers, so that, other things being equal, from their more
numerous ranks there would naturally come a larger number
of offenders against the law. But other things are not equal.
The proportion is not kept. Anyone who studies the police-
court reports in the local papers will see that, apart from cases
of technical offence, like riding a bicycle on the footpath, or
keeping a dog without a licence, practically all the proceedings
are taken in defence of the privileges and prejudices of the

employing classes against the employed classes. Clearly the village idea is not wholly wrong. In theory, the policeman represents the general public; in practice, he stands for middle-class decorum and the rights of property; and what the people say is roughly true—there is one law for the rich, and another for the poor.

But it is only roughly true, and one must get it a little more exact to appreciate the position in which the labouring-folk stand. I am not disposed to say anything here against the administration of the law by the justices, when offenders are brought before them; but in the choice or detection of offenders I must point out that a great deal of respect of persons is shown. Remember what that old man said, who would have liked to see the fir-woods go up in flames : " 'Tis all fenced in, and now if you looks over the fence you be locked up for it." That was an exaggeration, of course—a sort of artistic licence, a piece of oratory; yet for him the assertion held more than a grain of truth. The case is that of the two sorts of boys over again. Where a middle-class man may take his Sunday walk securely, risking nothing worse than being civilly turned back by a game-keeper, these village men dare not go, unless they are prepared to answer a summons for "trespassing for an unlawful pur-pose," or "in search of game." Let it be admitted that the unlawful purpose is sometimes proved; at least, the trespassers are occasionally found to have rabbit-wires concealed about their persons. The remarkable thing, however, is that they should have been searched in order to make this discovery. The searching may be legal, for all that I know; yet I do not seem to see a middle-class man—a shopkeeper from the town, or any employer of labour—submitting to the process, as the cowed labouring man apparently does. It will be said that the middle-class man is in no fear of such an outrage, because he is not suspect. But that is conceding the greater part of what I wish to demonstrate. Rightly or wrongly, the labouring man is suspect. A distinction of caste is made against him. The law, which pretends to impartiality, sets him in a lower and less privileged place than his employers; and he knows it. In alleging that he might not look over a fence without being locked up for it my old acquaintance merely overstated a palpable truth. People of his rank—cottage people, labouring people—do, indeed, not dare to wander in country places anywhere off the public roads.

Much more might be said on the same lines. Whether inevitably or no, at all events it happens that the march of respectability gives, to regulations which may be quite proper in themselves, a very strong appearance of being directed against the poorer working people. No doubt it is right enough that the brawling of the "drunk and disorderly" on the highroads should be checked; the public interest demands it; yet the impression conveyed is that the regulations are enforced more for the pleasure of property-owners than anybody else; that, in fact, middle-class respectability has, so to speak, made this law especially with a view to keeping the working classes in order. I am not urging that in this there is any substantial grievance; the offence is rarely committed by others than labourers, and by them too often. Yet it is well known that, while a labourer roystering along the road is pounced upon and locked up, an employer the worse for drink is shepherded home from his hotel by the police, and the affair hushed up. From circumstances like these—and they are very common —a suspicion is bred in cottage people that they are not in good odour with the authorities. The law rather tolerates than befriends them. They are not wanted, are not regarded as equal fellow-citizens with the well-to-do, but are expected to be quiet, or to keep out of sight. English people though they are, yet, if nobody will employ them so that they can pay rent for a cottage, they have no admitted rights in England—unless it be to go to the workhouse or to keep moving on upon the public road. In endless ways the sense of inequality is impressed upon them. I opened the local paper lately, and read of four of our young labourers accused of "card-playing." The game was "Banker," the policeman told the magistrates—as if gentlemen were likely to know what that meant!—and he had caught the fellows red-handed, in some as yet unfenced nook of the heath. That was how they were in fault. They should not have been playing where they could be seen, in the open air; they should have taken their objectionable game out of sight, into some private house, as the middle-classes do—and as, I suppose, the policeman himself must have done in his time, since he knew the game. Unfortunately for the labouring men, they have no private house available : there is no room for a card-party in their cottages; and thus they become subject to laws which, as they do not touch the property-owner, seem designed to catch especially them. For another example of the same insinuation of inequality, consider the local by-laws, which now forbid the keeping of pigs within a considerable distance of a dwelling-house. I will not say that the villager thinks the regulation a wrong one; at any rate he understands that it is excused in the interests of public health. But he also knows that it has been introduced since the arrival of middle-class people in the parish. They came, and his pigs had to go; so that in his eyes even the general public health looks like the health of rich residents rather than of poor ones.

The people display little resentment; they accept their position with equanimity. Nevertheless it drives them in upon themselves. Observing the conditions, and yielding to them as to something inherent in the nature of things, they strive to keep out of the way of the superior classes. They are an aloof population, though not as their ancestors were. They are fenced out from the country; they cannot with security go into enclosed wood or coppice; they must keep to the public way, and there they must behave so as not to disturb the employing classes. Accordingly, all up and down the valley they restrict themselves more and more soberly to their gardens and cottages, dreading few things so much as a collision with those impersonal forces which seem always to side with property and against people like them.

XIII

NOTICE TO QUIT

IT might be thought that at least when they are at home the people would be untroubled; yet that is not the case. Influences from the new civilization reach them in their cottages, and the intrusion is but the more searching for being impersonal.

It is borne in upon the senses in the shape of sights and sounds proclaiming across the valley that the village is an altered place, that the modern world is submerging it, that the old comfortable seclusion is gone. Even the obscurity of winter nights does not veil that truth; for where, but a few years ago, the quiet depths of darkness were but emphasized by a few glimmering cottage lights, there is now a more brilliant sparkling of lit-up villa windows, while northwards the sky has a dull glare from new road-lamps which line the ridge on its town side. As for the daytime, the labourer can hardly look from his door without seeing up or down the valley some sign or other telling of the invasion of a new people, unsympathetic to his order. He sees, and hears too. As he sweats at his gardening, the sounds of piano-playing come to him, or of the affected excitement of a tennis-party; or the braying of a motorcar informs him that the rich who are his masters are on the road. And though the man should go into his cottage and shut the door, these things must often have for him a sinister meaning which he cannot so easily shut out. There is a vague menace in them. They betoken to all the labouring people that their old home is no longer quite at their disposal, but is at the mercy of a new class who would willingly see their departure.

Perhaps the majority do not feel themselves personally threatened; nevertheless, the situation is disquieting for all. Before the property-owners came, and while still the population was homogeneous, a sort of continuity in the life of the valley impressed itself upon one's consciousness, giving a sense of security. Here amidst the heaths a laborious and frugal people, wise in their own fashion, had their home and supplied their own wants. Not one of them probably thought of the significance of it all, or understood how the village traditions were his inheritance; not one considered what it meant to him to belong to the little group of folk and be independent of the whims of strangers. Yet, for all that, there was comfort in the situation. To be so familiar as the people were with the peculiarities of the valley, to appreciate the usefulness of the wide heath-land, to value the weather, to comprehend at a glance the doings of the neighbours, and to have fellow-feeling with their motives and hopes and disappointments, was to be at home most intimately, most safely. But all this is a thing of the past. To-day, when the labourer looks around, much of what he sees in the new houses, roads, fences, and so on, has, indeed, been produced by his own handiwork, but it is a product in the enjoyment of which he has no share. It has nothing to do with him and his people; on the contrary, it announces the break-up of the traditional industries by which he lived, and the disintegration of the society of which he was a member. It follows that a certain suggestiveness which used to dignify the home pursuits of the village is wanting to them now. Instead of being a part of the general thrift of the valley —a not unworthy contribution to that which, in the sum, was all important to the village life—those little jobs which the labourer does at home, including his garden-work, have no relation now to anything save his private necessities, because now the dominant interests of the valley are those of a different sort of people who care nothing for such homely things. I shall be told that, after all, this is mere sentiment. But, then, half the comfort of life proceeds from those large vague sentiments which lift a man's private doings up from meanness into worthiness. No such enrichment, however—no dim sense of sharing in a prosperous and approved existence—can reward the labourer's industry in this place at the present time. The clever work which, in the village of his equals, would have made him conspicuous and respected, now stamps him as belonging to the least important and least considered section of the population.

Still, I will waive this point. Assuming—though it is much to assume—that the cottagers have no sentiment in the matter, there are other circumstances in the change which cannot fail to disquiet them. I hinted just now that the "residential" people would not grieve if the labouring folk took their departure. Now, this is no figure of speech. Although it is likely that not one cottager in twenty has any real cause to fear removal, there has been enough disturbance of the old families to prove that nobody is quite safe. Thus, about two years ago, when some cottage property near to a new "residence" was bought up by the owner of the residence, it was commonly said that he had bought it in order to get rid of some of the tenants, whom he disliked for neighbours. Whether or not that was the real reason I do not know; but certain it is that two of the tenants were forthwith turned out—one of them after twenty-five years of occupancy. It was not the first case of the kind in the village, nor yet the last. At the present moment I know of three families who are likely ere long to have to quit. They live in a block of cottages just beyond the hedge of a substantial house—a block which, it must be owned, is rather an eyesore from there, but which might easily be turned into a decent villa, and is actually up for sale for that purpose. And the dwellers in the substantial house are fervently hoping that a buyer of the cottages will soon come forward. They have told me so themselves. "Of course," they say, "we shall be sorry for the poor people to be turned out, but we should like to have nicer neighbours, of our own sort." So in their own valley these English people are not safe from molestation. With scarce more care for them than would be shown by a foreign invader, gentility pursues its ungentle aims. No cottager can feel quite secure. A dim uncertainty haunts the village, with noticeable effect upon everybody's activities. For a sort of calculating prudence is begotten of it, which is yet not thrift. It dissuades the people from working for a distant future. It cuts off hope, benumbs the tastes, paralyses the aspiration to beautify the home which may any day have to be abandoned.

And in the long run this effect, from which all the people suffer more or less unconsciously, is more injurious than the actual misfortune of having to move, which, after all, falls upon the few only. Not that I would make light of that calamity. Men under its shadow lie awake o' nights, worrying about it. While I am writing here, in a cottage near at hand there is a man under notice to quit, who is going through all the pitiful experiences—wondering where in the world he shall take his wife and children, fearing lest it should have to be into some backyard in the town, dreading that in that case he will be too far away from his day's work and have to give it up, and scheming to save enough, from the cost of bread and boots, to pay for a van to move his furniture. It is not for any fault that he is to go. And indeed he is being well treated; for the owner, who wants to occupy the cottage himself, has waited months because the man cannot find another place. Nevertheless he will have to go. As a rule, a man under notice to quit is in the position of standing by and seeing his home, and his living, and the well-being of his family sacrificed to the whim of a superior whom he dares not oppose; and I do not dream of arguing that that is a tolerable position for any Englishman to be in. None the less, it is true that these acute troubles, which fall upon a few people here and there, and presently are left

behind and forgotten, are of less serious import than the injury
to the village at large, caused by the general sense of insecurity.

The people's tastes are benumbed, I said: their aspirations
to beautify their homes are paralysed by the want of perma-
nence in their condition. To make this quite plain, it would
be only needful to look at the few cottages in the valley still
inhabited by their owners, and to compare them with those let
to weekly tenants. It seems to be no question of income that
makes the difference between the two. In several cottages very
well known to me, the owners are not earning more than fifteen shillings a week—or, including the value of the cottage,
twenty shillings; yet the places, in their varied ways, all look
comfortable and comely. Fruit-trees, or grape-vines, or roses,
are trained to the walls. The boundary hedges are kept well
trimmed; here and there survives a box border—product of
many years of clipping—or even a yew-tree or two fancifully
shaped out. Here and there, too, leading to the cottage door,
is carefully preserved an example of those neat pavements of
local stone once so characteristic of this countryside; and in all
these things one sees what the average cottager would do if it
were worth while—if he had the heart. Since none of these
things, however, can be had without long attention, or, at any
rate, without skill carefully bestowed in due season, you do not
find such things decorating the homes of weekly tenants. The
cottages let by the week look shabby, slovenly, dingy; the
hedges of the gardens are neglected, broken down, stopped up
with anything that comes to hand. If it were not for the
fruitful and well-tended vegetable plots, one might often suppose the tenants to be ignorant of order, degenerate, brutalized,
materialized, so sordid and ugly are their homes.

Yet it is not for want of taste that they endure these conditions. Amidst the pitiful shabbiness which prevails may be
found many little signs that the delight in comely things would
go far if it dared. There is hardly a garden in the village, I
think, which does not contain a corner or a strip given over

unthriftily, not to useful vegetables, but to daffodils or carnations or dahlias, or to the plants of sweet scent and pleasant names, like rosemary and lavender, and balm, and mignonette. And not seldom a weekly tenant, desirous of beauty, goes farther, takes his chance of losing his pains; nails up against his doorway some makeshift structure of fir-poles to be a porch, sowing nasturtiums or sweet-peas to cover it with their short-lived beauty; or he marks out under his window some little trumpery border to serve instead of a box-hedge as safeguard to his flowers. One of those families whose removal was mentioned above—turned out in the summer-time they were, with loss of garden crops—found refuge in a hovel which stood right against a public pathway. And, although it was an encroachment, within a week a twelve-inch strip of the pathway was dug up under the cottage eaves, and fenced in with a low fencing of sticks roughly nailed together. Within this narrow space were planted chrysanthemums rescued from the previous home; and when the fence gave way—as it did before the chrysanthemums flowered—big stones and brickbats were laid in its place. Considered as a decoration, the result was a failure; it was the product of an hour's work in which despair and bitterness had all but killed the people's hope; but that it was done at all is almost enough to prove my point. For further illustration I may refer again to that other man mentioned above, who is now under notice to leave his cottage. Last year he was happy in tending four or five rose-trees which he had been allowed to bring home from the rubbish-heap of his employer's garden. I remember that when he showed them to me, gloating over them, he tried to excuse himself to me for neglecting his potatoes in their favour, and I did my best to encourage him and puff him up with pride. But it was of no use. This summer he is neglecting his roses, and is wondering if his potatoes will be ripe enough for digging before he is obliged to move.

With such things going on, it is not wonderful that the

people live shabbily, meanly, out at elbows. Tastes so handi-capped as theirs make no headway, and, though not dying, sink into disuse. The average cottager learns to despise pleasant-ness and to concentrate upon usefulness. His chief pride now is in his food-crops, which, if not eaten, can be turned into money. Of course, these have their beauty—not undiscerned by the labourer—but they are not grown for that end, and the thriftier the man, the less time to the consideration of beauty will he give. It is, besides, an imprudence to make a cottage look comely, now that covetous eyes are upon the valley and the people's position there has grown insecure.

Does it seem a slight thing? Whatever the practical impor-tance of it, the extent of change involved in this hopeless atti-tude of the villagers towards their home-places must not be underrated; for if it could be viewed in sharp perspective it would appear considerable enough. Let us note the transitions. First the straying squatters settled here, to cultivate chosen spots of the valley and reduce them to order. They were not wedded to the place; only if it gave them a chance of getting food and shelter were they likely to remain. Soon, however, that first uncertainty was forgotten. Their peasant customs fitted the environment; there was no danger of molestation; already to their children the valley began to feel like a per-manent home. As years went on that feeling deepened, wrapped the people round in an unthought-of security, and permitted them, here and there, to go beyond the necessary peasant crafts and think of what was pleasant as well as neces-sary. Gardens were trimmed into beauty, grape-vines were grown for the sake of wine-making, and bees were kept for the sake of honey and mead. In the cottages decent furniture and implements began to accumulate; the women decorated their men's blouses with pretty smocking; the children were taught old-fashioned lore because it was old-fashioned and their inheritance; time-honoured customs of May-day and of Christ-

country thrift and its simple civilization were kept alive, until the loss of the common made the old thrift no longer possible and introduced the new. Lastly, and within recent years, a new population has come, taking possession, with a new civilization which is by no means simple; and now once more a sense of unsettledness is upon the cottagers, although for the most part they remain here. It is, however, an unsettledness very unlike that of the earlier time. Instead of hope in it there is anxiety; instead of striking deeper root in the valley, the people's hold grows shallower. The agreeable peasant arts have faded out accordingly. The whole peasant mode of life is all but forgotten. To-day we have here not a distinct group of people living by customs which their singular circumstances justify, but numerous impoverished families living provisionally from hand to mouth, because of the possibility of further changes to be thrust upon them. While they wait they still work, yet without pleasantness in their lives. As their homes by neglect have grown shabby and squalid, so their industry has become calculating and sordid. Little remains to them now but their own good temper to keep their life from being quite joyless.

IV

THE RESULTING NEEDS

XIV

THE INITIAL DEFECT

KEEPING pace with the alterations in their circumstances, a great mental and spiritual destitution has made its appearance amongst the labouring people. I say "has made its appearance" because it cannot be wholly attributed to the changes we have been discussing. Those changes have done their part, certainly. Obliterating the country crafts and cults, breaking down the old neighbourly feelings, turning what was an interesting economy into an anxious calculation of shillings and pence, and reducing a whole village of people from independence to a position bordering on servility, the introduction of a new system of thrift must bear the greater share of the blame for the present plight of the labourers. Nevertheless, their destitution—their mental and spiritual destitution—has its roots deeper down, and springs from a grave defect which was inherent in the peasant system. It is time to recognize that fact. In many ways the folk-civilization had served the cottagers excellently. They had grown up hardy and self-reliant under its influence; clever with their hands, shrewd with their heads, kindly and cheerful in their temper. But one can see now that all this has been bought very dear. To set against the good qualities that came to light there was a stifling of other qualities which were equally good, but had no chance of development at all under the peasant thrift.

Especially on the side of mental activity was the people's natural power cramped. I do not mean that they were stupid; it would be an error of the first magnitude to suppose anything of the sort. But the concentration of their faculties on their rural doings left them childish and inefficient in the use of their brains for other purposes. Mention has been made of the "fatalism" which still prevails in the village outlook; but fatalism is too respectable a name for that mere absence of speculative thought which was characteristic of the peasant kind of people I have known. The interest of their daily pursuits kept their minds busy upon matters obvious to the senses, while attention to opinions and ideas was discouraged. For this reason the older men and women had seldom if ever indulged in fancies or day-dreams, or troubled about theories or first principles; and until lately I might have said the same of the younger ones too. As for watching themselves—watching and checking off the actions of their own intelligence—it was what they never did. A sentiment might arise in them and mellow all their temper, and they would not notice it. The inner meaning of things concerned them very little. Their conception of cause and effect, or of the constancy of nature, was rudimentary. "Ninety-nine times out of a hundred," said an old bricklayer of the village, baffled by some error in his work—"ninety-nine times out of a hundred it'll come right same as you sets it out, but not always." Puzzles were allowed to be puzzling, and left so; or the first explanation was accepted as final. The "mistis in March" sufficiently accounted for the "frostis in May." Mushrooms would only grow when the moon was "growing." Even with regard to personal troubles the people were still as unspeculative as ever. Were they poor, or ill? It merely happened so, and that settled it. Or were they in cheerful spirits? Why, so they were; and what more could be said?

It was largely this simplicity of their mental processes that made the older people so companionable. They were unaccustomed to using certain powers of the brain which modern people use; nay, they were so unaware of that use as to be utterly unsuspicious of such a thing. To be as little psychological as possible, we may say that a modern man's thought goes on habitually at two main levels. On the surface are the subjects of the moment—that endless procession of things seen or heard or spoken of which make up the outer world; and here is where intercourse with the old type of villager was easy and agreeable. But below that surface the modern mind has a habit of interpreting these phenomena by general ideas or abstract principles, or referring them to imaginations all out of sight and unmentioned; and into this region of thought the peasant's attention hardly penetrated at all. Given a knowledge of the neighbourhood, therefore, it was easy to keep conversation going with a man of this kind. If you could find out the set of superficial or practical subjects in which he was interested, and chatter solely on that plane, all went well. But if you dipped underneath it amongst fancies or generalizations, difficulties arose. The old people had no experience there, and were out of their depth in a moment. And yet—I must repeat it—we should be entirely wrong to infer that they were naturally stupid, unless a man is to be called stupid because he does not cultivate every one of his inborn faculties. In that sense we all have our portion in stupidity, and the peasant was no worse than the rest of us. His particular deficiency was as I have described it, and may be fully explained by his mode of life. For in cow-stall or garden or cottage, or in the fields or on the heaths, the claim of the moment was all-absorbing; and as he hurried to thatch his rick before the rain came, or to get his turfs home by nightfall, the ideas which thronged about his doings crowded out ideas of any other sort. Or if, not hurrying, his mind went dreamy, it was still of peasant things that he dreamed. Of what he had been told when he was a child, or what he had seen for himself in after-life, his memory was full; and every stroke of reap-hook or thrust of spade had power to entice his intellect along the familiar grooves of thought—grooves which lie on the surface and are unconnected with any systematized channels of idea-work underneath.

So the strong country life tyrannized over country brains, and, apart from the ideas suggested by that life, the peasant folk had few ideas. Their minds lacked freedom; there was no escape from the actual environment into a world either of imagination or of more scientific understanding. Nor did this matter a great deal, so long as the environment remained intact. In the absence of what we call " views "—those generalizations about destiny or goodness, or pleasure, or what not, by which we others grope our way through life—the steady peasant environment, so well known and containing so few surprises, was itself helpful, precisely because it was so well known. If a man would but give shrewd attention to his practical affairs, it was enough; a substitute for philosophy was already made for him, to save him the trouble of thinking things out for himself. His whole mental activity proceeded, unawares, upon a substratum of customary understanding, which belonged to the village in general, and did not require to be formulated, but was accepted as axiomatic by all. " Understanding " is the best word I can find for it. It differed from a philosophy or a belief, because it contained no abstract ideas; thinking or theorizing had no part in it; it was a sheer perception and recognition of the circumstances as they were. The people might dispute about details; but the general object to be striven for in life admitted of no disagreement. Without giving it a thought, they knew it. There lay the valley before them, with their little homesteads, their cattle, their gardens, the common; and connected with all these things a certain old-established series of industries was recognized, leading up to a well-known prosperity. That perception was their philosophy. The environment was understood through and through. And this common knowledge, existing apart from any individual in particular, served every individual instead of a set of private opinions of his own. To get away from it was impossible, for it was real knowledge; a man's practical thoughts had to harmonize with it; supported by it, he was saved the trouble of thinking things out in " systems "; and in fact it was a better guide to him than thought-out systems could have been, because generations of experience had fitted it so perfectly to the narrow environment of the valley. So long, therefore, as the environment remained unaltered, the truth that the people's minds held few ideas upon other subjects, and had developed no method of systematic thinking, was veiled.

But it has become plain enough now that the old environment is gone. The new thrift has laid bare the nakedness of the land. It has found the villagers unequipped with any efficient mental habits appropriate to the altered conditions, and shown them to be at a loss for interesting ideas in other directions. They cannot see their way any longer. They have no aims at any rate, no man is sure what his own aims ought to be, or has any confidence that his neighbours could enlighten him. Life has grown meaningless, stupid; an apathy reigns in the village—a dull waiting, with nothing in particular for which to wait.

XV

THE OPPORTUNITY

AMONGST so many drawbacks to the new thrift, one good thing that it has brought to the villagers, in the shape of a little leisure, gives us the means of seeing in more detail how destitute of interests their life has become. It must be owned that the leisure is very scanty. It is so obscured, too, by the people's habit of putting themselves to productive work in it that I have sometimes doubted if any benefit of the kind actually filtered down into their overburdened lives. Others, however, with a more business-like interest in the matter than mine, have recognized that a new thing has come into the country labourer's life, although they do not speak of it as "leisure." Mere wasted time is what it looks like to them. Thus, not long ago, an acquaintance who by no means shares my views of these matters was deploring to me the degenerate state, as he conceived it, of the labourers on certain farms in which he is interested, a few miles away from this valley. The men, he said, holding their cottages as one of the conditions of employment on the farms, had grown idle, and were neglecting the cottage gardens—were neglecting them so seriously that, in the interests of the estate, he had been obliged to complain to the farmers. Upon my asking for explanations of a disposition so unlike that of the labourers in this parish, many of whom are not content with their cottage gardens, but take more ground when they can get it, my friend said deliberately: "I think food is too cheap. With their fifteen shillings a week the men can buy all they want without working for it; and the result is that they waste their evenings and the gardens go to ruin."

With this remarkable explanation I am glad to think that I have nothing to do here. The point is that, according to a business man with lifelong experience in rural matters, country labourers now have time at their disposal. Without further question we may accept it as true; the cheapening of produce has made it just possible for labouring men to live without occupying every available hour in productive work, and in this one respect they do profit a little by those innovations—the use of machinery, the division of labour, and the free importation of foreign goods—which have replaced the antiquated peasant economy. It is not necessary nowadays—not absolutely necessary—for the labourer, when his day's wage-earning is done, to fall to work again in the evening in order to produce commodities for his own use. Doubtless if he does so he is the better off; but if he fails to do so he may still live. While he has been earning money away from home during the day, other men he has never met, in countries he has never seen, have been providing for him the things that he will want at home in the evening; and if these things have not been actually brought to his door, they are waiting for him in shops, whence he may get them in exchange for the money he has earned. Some of them, too, are of a quality such as, with the utmost skill and industry, he never could have produced for himself. Modern artificial light provides an example. Those home-made rush-lights eulogized by Gilbert White and by Cobbett may have been well enough in their way, but cheap lamps and cheap paraffin have given the villagers their winter evenings. At a cost of a few halfpence earned in the course of the day's work a cottage family may prolong their winter's day as far into the night as they please; and that, without feeling that they are wasting their store of light, and without being under the necessity of spending the rescued hours at any of those thrifty tasks which alone would have justified peasant folk in sitting up late. They have the evening to use at their pleasure.

If it is said, as my friend interested in land seemed to suggest, that they do not know how to use it, I am not concerned to disagree. In fact, that is my own text. On an evening last winter, having occasion to ask a neighbour to do me a service, I knocked at his cottage door, and was invited in. The unshaded lamp on the table cast a hard, strong light on the appointments of the room, and in its glare the family—namely, the man, with his wife, his mother, and his sister—were sitting round the fire. On the table, which had no cloth, the remains of his hot tea-supper were not cleared away—the crust of a loaf, a piece of bacon-rind on a plate, and a teacup showed what it had been. But now he had finished, and was resting in his shirt-sleeves, nursing his baby. In fact, the evening's occupation had begun. The family, that is to say, had two or three hours to spend—for it was but little past seven o'clock—and nothing to do but to sit there and gossip. An innocent pastime that; I have no fault to find with it, excepting that it had the appearance of being very dull. The people looked comfortable, but there was no liveliness in them. No trace of vivacity in their faces gave the smallest reason to suppose that my coming had interrupted any enjoyment of the evening. A listless contentment in being at home together, with the day's work done and a fire to sit by, was what was suggested by the whole bearing of the family. Their leisure was of no use to them for recreation—for "making themselves anew," that is—or for giving play to faculties which had lain quiet during the day's work. At the time, however, I saw nothing significant in all this. It was just what other cottage interiors had revealed to me on other winter evenings. The surprising, the unexpected thing would have been to find the little spell of leisure being joyfully used.

Shall we leave the matter there then? If we do, we shall overlook the one feature in the situation that most particularly deserves attention. For suppose that the cottagers in general do not know what to do with their leisure, yet we must not argue that therefore they do not prize it. Dull though they may seem in it, tedious though I believe they often find it, nevertheless there proceeds from it a subtle satisfaction, as at something gained, in the liberty to behave as they like, in the vague sense that for an hour or two no further effort is demanded of them. Yawning for bed, half sick of the evening, somewhere in the back of their consciousness they feel that this respite from labour, which they have won by the day's work, is a privilege not to be thrown away. It is more to them than a mere cessation from toil, a mere interval between more important hours; it is itself the most important part of the day —the part to which all the rest has led up.

Nothing of the sort, I believe, was experienced in the village in earlier times. Leisure, and the problem of using it, are new things there. I do not mean that the older inhabitants of the valley never had any spare time. There were, doubtless, many hours when they "eased off," to smoke their pipes and drink their beer and be jolly; only, such hours were, so to speak, a by-product of living, not the usual and expected consummation of every day. Accepting them by no means unwillingly when they occurred, the folk still were wont normally to reduce them to a minimum, or at least to see that they did not occur too often; as if spare time, after all, was only a time of waiting until work could be conveniently resumed. So lightly was it valued that most villagers cut it short by the simple expedient of going to bed at six or seven o'clock. But then, in their peasant way, they enjoyed interesting days. The work they did, although it left their reasoning and imaginative powers undeveloped, called into play enough subtle knowledge and skill to make their whole day's industry gratifying. What should they want of leisure? They wanted rest, in which to recover strength for taking up again the interesting business of living; but they approached their daily life—their pig-keeping and bread-making, their mowing and thatching and turf-cutting and gardening, and the whole round of country tasks —almost in a welcoming spirit, matching themselves against its demands and proving their manhood by their success. But the modern labourer's employment, reduced as it is to so much greater monotony, and carried on for a master instead of for the man himself, is seldom to be approached in that spirit. The money-valuation of it is the prime consideration; it is a commercial affair; a clerk going to his office has as much reason as the labourer to welcome the morning's call to work. As in the clerk's case, so in the labourer's: the act or fruition of living is postponed during the hours in which the living is being earned; between the two processes a sharp line of division is drawn; and it is not until the clock strikes, and the leisure begins, that a man may remember that he is a man, and try to make a success of living. Hence the truth of what I say: the problem of using leisure is a new one in the village. Deprived, by the economic changes which have gone over them, of any keen enjoyment of life while at work, the labourers must make up for the deprivation when work is over, or not at all. Naturally enough, in the absence of any traditions to guide them, they fail. But self-respect forbids the old solution. To feed and go to bed would be to shirk the problem, not to solve it.

So much turns upon a proper appreciation of these truths that it will be well to illustrate them from real life, contrasting the old against the new. Fortunately the means are available. Modernized people acquainted with leisure are in every cottage, while as for the others, the valley still contains a few elderly men whose lives are reminiscent of the earlier day. Accordingly I shall finish this chapter by giving an account of one of these latter, so that in the next chapter the different position of the present-day labourers may be more exactly understood.

The man I have in mind—I will rename him Turner—belongs to one of the old families of the village, and inherited from his father a cottage and an acre or so of ground—probably mortgaged—together with a horse and cart, a donkey, a cow or two, a few pigs, and a fair stock of the usual rustic tools and implements. Unluckily for him, he inherited no traditions —there were none in his family—to teach him how to use these possessions for making a money profit; so that, trying to go on in the old way, as if the world were not changing all round him, he muddled away his chances, and by the time that he was fifty had no property left that was worth any creditor's notice. The loss, however, came too late to have much effect on his habits. And now that he is but the weekly tenant of a tiny cottage, and owns no more than a donkey and cart and a few rabbits and fowls, he is just the same sort of man that he used to be in prosperity—thriftless from our point of view, but from the peasant point of view thrifty enough, good-tempered too, generous to a fault, indifferent to discomforts, as a rule very hard-working, yet apparently quite unacquainted with fatigue.

He gets his living now as a labourer; but, unlike his neighbours, he seems by no means careful to secure constant employment. The regularity of it would hardly suit his temper;

he is too keenly desirous of being his own master. And his own master he manages to be, in a certain degree. From those who employ him he obtains some latitude of choice, not alone as to the hours of the day when he shall serve them, but even as to the days of the week. I have heard him protest : " Monday you says for me to come. Well, I dunno about *Monday*— if Tuesday'd suit ye as well? I wants to do so-and-so o' Monday, if 'tis fine. You see, there's Mr. S—— I bin so busy I en't bin anear him this week for fear *he* should want me up *there*. I *knows* his grass wants cuttin'. But I 'xpects I shall ha' to satisfy 'n Monday, or else p'raps he won't like it." Sometimes he takes a day for his own affairs, carting home hop-bine in his donkey-cart, or getting heath for some thatching job that has been offered to him. On these terms, while he finds plenty to do in working intermittently for four or five people in the parish, he preserves a freedom of action which probably no other labourer in the village enjoys. Few others could command it. But Turner's manner is so ingratiating that people have a personal liking for him, and it is certain that his strength and all-round handiness make of him an extremely useful man. Especially does his versatility commend him. Others in the village are as strong as he and as active and willing, but there are not now many others who can do such a number of different kinds of work as he can, with so much experienced readiness.

Among his clients (for that is a more fitting word for them than " employers ") there are two or three residents with villa gardens, and also two of those " small-holders " who, more fortunate than himself (though not more happy, I fancy), have managed to cling to the little properties which their fathers owned. Turner, therefore, comes in for a number of jobs extraordinarily diverse. Thus, during last summer I knew him to be tending two gardens, where his work ranged from lawn-cutting (sometimes with a scythe) to sowing seeds, taking care of the vegetable crops, and trimming hedges. But this occupied him only from seven in the morning until five in the afternoon. In the margin outside these hours—starting at five or earlier and keeping on until dark—he was helping the two small-holders, one after the other, to make their hay and get the ricks built. Then the ricks required thatching, and Turner thatched them. In the meantime he was getting together a little rick of his own for his donkey's use, carrying home in bags the longer grass which he had mowed in the rough places of people's gardens or had chopped off in hedgerows near his home. A month later he was harvesting for the smallholders, and again there was rick-thatching for him to do. "That's seven I've done," he remarked to me, on the day when he finished the last one. "But didn't the rain stop you this morning?" I asked, for rain had begun heavily about nine o'clock. He laughed. "No . . . We got'n covered in somehow. Had to scramble about, but he was thatched afore the rain come."

Later still he was threshing some of this corn with a flail. I heard of it with astonishment. "A flail?" "Yes," he said; "my old dad put me to it when I was seventeen, so I *had* to learn." He seemed to think little of it. But to me threshing by hand was so obsolete and antiquated a thing as to be a novelty; nor yet to me only, for a friend to whom I mentioned the matter laughed, and asked if I had come across any knights in armour lately.

One autumn, when he was doing some work for myself, he begged for a day or two away in order to take a job at turf-cutting. When he returned on the third or fourth day, he said: "Me and my nipper" (a lad of about sixteen years old) "cut sixteen hundred this time." Now, lawn-turfs are cut to a standard size, three feet by one, wherefore I remarked: "Why, that's nearly a mile you have cut." "Oh, is it?" he said. "But it didn't take long. Ye see, I had the nipper to go along with the edgin' tool in front of me, and 'twan't much trouble to get 'em up."

He could not keep on for me regularly. The thought of

Mr. S——'s work waiting to be done fidgeted him. "When I was up there last he was talkin' about fresh gravellin' all his paths. I said to'n, 'If I was you I should wait anyhow till the leaves is down—they'll make the new gravel so ontidy else.' So they would, sure. I keeps puttin' it off. But I shall ha' to go. I sold'n a little donkey in the summer, and he's hoofs'll want parin' again. I done 'em not so long ago. . . ."

So his work varies, week after week. From one job to another up and down the valley he goes, not listlessly and fatigued, but taking a sober interest in all he does. You can see in him very well how his forefathers went about their affairs, for he is plainly a man after their pattern. His day's work is his day's pleasure. It is changeful enough, and calls for skill enough, to make it enjoyable to him. Furthermore, things on either side of it—things he learnt to understand long ago—make their old appeal to his senses as he goes about, although his actual work is not concerned with them. In the early summer—he had come to mow a little grass plot for me—I found him full of a boyish delight in birds and birds'-nests. A pair of interesting birds had arrived; at any time in the day they could be seen swooping down from the branch of a certain apple-tree and back again to their starting-place without having touched the ground. "Fly-catchers!" said Turner exultantly. "I shall ha' to look about. They got their nest somewhere near, you may be sure o' that! A little wisp o' grass somewhere in the clunch (fork) of a tree . . ." (his glance wandered speculatively round in search of a likely place) "that's where they builds. Ah! look now! There he goes again! Right in the clunch you'll find their nest, and as many as ten young 'uns in'n. . . . Yes, I shall be bound to find where he is afore I done with it."

The next day, hard by where he was at work, an exclamation of mine drew him to look at a half-fledged bird, still alive, lying at the foot of a nut-tree. "H'm: so 'tis. A young blackbird," he said pitifully. The next moment he had the bird in his hand. "Where can the nest be, then? Up in that nut? Well, to be sure! Wonders I hadn't seen that afore now. That's it though, 'pend upon it; right up in the clunch o' that bough." Before I could say a word he was half-way up amongst the branches, long-legged and struggling, to put the bird back into its nest.

As he has always lived in the valley, he is full of memories of it, and especially early memories; recalling the comparative scantiness of its population when he was a boy, and the great extent of the common; and the warm banks where hedgehogs abounded—hedgehogs which his father used to kill and cook; and the wells of good water, so few and precious that each had its local name. For instance, " Butcher's Well " (so-called to this day, he says) " was where Jack Butcher used to live, what was shepherd for Mr. Warner up there at Manley Bridge." At eight years old he was sent out on to the common to mind cows; at ten he was thought big enough to be helpful to his father, at piece-work in the hop-grounds; and in due time he began to go " down into Sussex " with his father and others for the harvesting. His very first experience there was of a wet August, when the men could earn no money and were reduced to living on bread and apples; but other years have left him with happier memories of that annual outing. "Old Sussex!" he laughed once in appreciative reminiscence—"Old Sussex! Them old hills! I did use to have a appetite there! I could eat anything. . . . You could go to the top of a hill and look down one way and p'raps not see more'n four or five places (houses or farmsteads), and look t'other way and mebbe not be able to see e'er a one at all. Oh, a reg'lar wild, out-o'-th'-way place 'twas." On this farm, to which his gang went year after year, the farmer " didn't *pay* very high—you couldn't expect'n to. But he used to treat us very well. Send out great puddin's for us two or three times a week, and cider, and bread-an'-cheese. . . . Nine rabbits old Fisher the roadman out here says 'twas, but I dunno 'bout that, but I *knows* 'twas as many

as seven, the farmer put into one puddin' for us. There was
a rabbit for each man, be how 'twill. In a great yaller
basin. . . ." Turner held out his arms to illustrate a large cir-
cumference.

In the time of his prosperity the main of his work was with
his own horse and cart, so that I know him to have had considerable experience in that way; and I recollect, too, his being
at plough in one of the slanting gardens of this valley, not with
his horse—the ground was too steep for that—but with two
donkeys harnessed to a small plough which he kept especially
for such work. Truly it would be hard to " put him out," hard
to find him at a loss, in anything connected with country industry. He spoilt some sea-kale for me once, admitting, however, before he began that he was not very familiar with its
management; but that is the only matter of its kind in which
I have proved him inefficient. To see him putting young
cabbage-plants in rows is to realize what a fine thing it is to
know the best way of going to work, even at such a simple-
seeming task as that; and I would not undertake to count in
how many such things he is proficient.

One day he was telling me an anecdote of his taking honey
from an old-fashioned straw beehive; another day the talk was
of pruning fruit-trees. I had shown him an apple—the first
one to be picked from a young tree—and he at once named it
correctly as a " Blenheim Orange," recognizing it by its "eye,"
whereupon I asked a question or two, and, finally, if he understood pruning. There came his customary laugh, while his
eyes twinkled, as if the question amused him, as if I might
have known that he understood pruning. " Yes, I've done it
many's a time. Grape vines, too." Who taught him? " Oh,
'twas my old uncle made me do that. He was laid up one
time—'twas when I was eighteen year old—and he says to me:
' You'll ha' to do it. Now's your time to learn. . . .' Of
course he showed me *how*. So 'twas he as showed me how to
thatch. . . . My father never knowed how to do thatchin',

nor anythink else much. He was mostly hop-ground. He done a little mowin', of course." Equally, of course, the father had reaped and harvested, and kept pigs and cows, and a few odd things besides; nevertheless, being chiefly a wage-earner, " he never knowed much," and it was to the uncle that the lad owed his best training.

From talk of the uncle, and of the uncle's cows, of which he had charge for a time, he drifted off to mention a curious piece of old thrift connected with the common, and practised apparently for some time after the enclosure. There was a man he knew in those now remote days who fed his cows for a part of the year on furze, or " fuzz," as we call it here. Two acres of furze he had, which he cut close in alternate years, the second year's growth making a fine juicy fodder when chopped small into a sort of chaff. An old hand-apparatus for that purpose— a kind of chaff-cutting box—was described to me. The same man had a horse, which also did well on furze diet mixed with a little malt from the man's own beer-brewing.

To the lore derived from his uncle and others, Turner has added much by his own observation—not, of course, intentional observation scientifically verified, but that shrewd and practical folk-observation, if I may so call it, by which in the course of generations the rural English had already garnered such a store of mingled knowledge and error. So he knows, or thinks he knows, why certain late-bearing apple-trees have fruit only every other year, and what effect on the potato crop is caused by dressing our sandy soil with chalk or lime; so he watches the new mole-runs, or puzzles to make out what birds they can be that peck the ripening peas out of the pods, or estimates the yield of oats to the acre by counting the sheaves that he stacks, or examines the lawn to see what kinds of grass are thriving. About all such matters his talk is the talk of an experienced man habitually interested in his subject, and yet it is never obtrusive. The remarks fall from him casually; you feel, too, that while he is telling you something that he noticed yesterday or years ago his eyes are alert to seize any new detail that may seem worthy of attention. Details are always really his subject, for the generalizations he sometimes offers are built on the flimsiest foundation of but one or two observed facts. But I am not now concerned with the value of his observations for themselves; the point is that to him they are so interesting. He is a man who seems to enjoy his life with an undiminished zest from morning to night. It is doubtful if the working hours afford, to nine out of ten modern and even " educated " men, such a constant refreshment of acceptable incidents as Turner's hours bring to him.

He is perhaps the best specimen of the old stock now left in the valley; but it must not be thought that he is singular. Others there are not very unlike him; and all that one hears of them goes to prove that the old cottage thrift, whatever its limitations may have been, did at least make the day's work interesting enough to a man, without his needing to care about leisure evenings. Turner, for his part, does not value them at all. In the winter he is often in bed before seven o'clock.

XVI

THE OBSTACLES

KEEPING this old-fashioned kind of life in mind as we turn again to the modern labourer's existence, we see at once where the change has come in, and why leisure, from being of small account, has become of so great importance. It is the amends due for a deprivation that has been suffered. Unlike the industry of a peasantry, commercial wage-earning cannot satisfy the cravings of a man's soul at the same time that it occupies his body, cannot exercise many of his faculties or appeal to many of his tastes; and therefore, if he would have any profit, any enjoyment, of his own human nature, he must contrive to get it in his leisure time.

In illustration of this position, I will take the case—it is fairly typical—of the coal-carter mentioned in the last chapter. He is about twenty-five years old now; and his career so far, from the time when he left school, may be soon outlined. It is true, I cannot say what his first employment was; but it can be guessed; for there is no doubt that he began as an errand-boy, and that presently, growing bigger, he took a turn at driving a gravel-cart to and fro between the gravel-pits and the railway. Assuming this, I can go on to speak from my own knowledge. His growth and strength came early; I remember noticing him first as a powerful fellow, not more than seventeen or eighteen years old, but already doing a man's work as a gravel-digger. When that work slackened after two or three years, he got employment—not willingly, but because times were bad—at night-work with the " ballast-train " on the railway. Exhausting if not brutalizing labour, that is. At ten or eleven at night the gangs of men started off, travelling in open trucks to the part of the line they are to repair, and there they work throughout the night, on wind-swept embankment or in draughty cutting, taking all the weather that the nights bring up. This man endured it for some twelve months, until a neglected chill turned to bronchitis and pleurisy, and nearly ended his life. After that he had a long spell of unemployment, and was on the point of going back to the ballast-train as a last resource when, by good fortune, he got his present job. He has been a coal-carter for three or four years—a fact which testifies to his efficiency. By half-past six o'clock in the morning he has to be in the stables; then comes the day on the road, during which he will lift on his back, into the van and out of it, and perhaps will carry for long distances, nine or ten tons of coal—say, twenty hundredweight bags every hour; by half-past five or six in the evening he has put up his horse for the night; and so his day's work is over, excepting that he has about a mile to walk home.

Of this employment, which, if the man is lucky, will continue until he is old and worn-out, we may admit that it is more useful by far—to the community—than the old village industries were wont to be. Concentrated upon one kind of effort, it perhaps doubles the productivity of a day's work. But just because it is so concentrated it cannot yield to the man himself any variety of delights such as men occupied in the old way were wont to enjoy. It demands from him but little skill; it neither requires him to possess a great fund of local information and useful lore, nor yet takes him where he could gather such a store for his own pleasure. The zest and fascination of living, with the senses alert, the tastes awake, and manifold sights and sounds appealing to his happy recognition—all these have to be forgotten until he gets home and is free for a little while. Then he may seek them if he can, using art or pastimes —what we call "civilization"—for that end. The two hours or so of leisure are his opportunity.

But after a day like the coal-carter's, where is the man that could even begin to refresh himself with the arts, or even the games, of civilization? For all the active use he can make of them those spare hours of his do not deserve to be called leisure; they are the fagged end of the day. Slouching home to them, as it were from under ten tons of coal, he has no energy left for further effort. The community has had all his energy, all his power to enjoy civilization; and has paid him three shillings and sixpence for it. It is small wonder that he seems not to avail himself of the opportunity, prize it though he may.

Yet there is still a possibility to be considered. Albeit any active use of leisure is out of the question, is he therefore debarred from a more tranquil enjoyment? He sits gossiping with his family, but why should the gossip be listless and yawning? Why should not he, to say nothing of his relations, enjoy the refreshment of talk enlivened by the play of pleasant and varied thoughts As everyone knows, the actual topic of conversation is not what makes the charm; be what it may, it will still be agreeable, provided that it goes to an accompaniment of ideas too plentiful and swift to be expressed. Every allusion then extends the interest of it; reawakened memories add to its pleasure; if the minds engaged are fairly well furnished with ideas, either by experience or by education, the intercourse between them goes on in a sort of luminous medium which fills the whole being with contentment. Supposing, then, that by education, or previous experience, the coal-carter's mind has been thus well furnished, his scanty leisure may still compensate him for the long dull hours of his wage-earning, and the new thrift will after all have made amends for the deprivation of the old peasant enjoyments.

But to suppose this is to suppose a most unlikely thing. Previous experience, at any rate, has done little for the man. The peasants themselves were better off. Compare his chances, once more, with those of a man like Turner. From earliest childhood, Turner's days and nights have been bountiful to him in many-coloured impressions. At the outset he saw and had part in those rural activities, changeful, accomplished, carried on by many forms of skill and directed by a vast amount of traditional wisdom, whereby the country people of England had for ages supported themselves in their quiet valleys. His brain still teems with recollections of all this industry. And then to those recollections must be added memories of the scenes in which the industry went on—the wide landscapes, the glowing cornfields, the meadows, woods, heaths; and likewise the ·details· of barn and rick-yard, and stable and cowstall, and numberless other corners into which his work has taken him. To anyone who understands them, those details are themselves like an interesting book, full of " idea " legible everywhere in the shapes which country craftsmanship gave to them; and Turner understands them through and through. Nor is this all. If not actual adventure and romance, still many of the factors of adventure and romance have accompanied him through his life; so that it is good even to think of all that he has seen. He has had experience (travelling down to Sussex) of the dead silence of country roads at midnight under the stars; has known the August sunrise, and the afternoon heat, and the chilly moonlight, high up on the South Downs; and the glint of the sunshine in apple-orchards at cider-making time; and the grey coming of the rain that urges a man to hurry with his thatching; and the thickening of the white winter fog across the heaths towards night-fall, when wayfarers might miss the track and wander all night unless they knew well what they were about. Of such stuff as this for the brain-life to feed upon there has been great abundance in Turner's career, but of such stuff what memories can the coal-carter have?

Already in his earliest childhood the principal chances were gone. The common had been enclosed; no little boys were sent out to mind cows there all day, and incidentally to look for birds'-nests and acquaint themselves with the ways of the rabbits and hedgehogs and butterflies and birds of the heath. Fenced-in property, guarded by the Policeman and the Law, restricted the boy's games to the shabby waste-places of the valley, and to the footpaths and roads, where there was not much for a child to do or to see. At home, and in the homes of his companions, the new thrift was in vogue; he might not watch the homely cottage doings, and listen to traditional talk about them, and look up admiringly at able men and women engaged upon them, for the very good reason that no such things went on. Men slaving at their gardens he might see, and women weary at their washing and mending, amid scenes of little dignity and much poverty and makeshift untidiness; but that was all. The coherent and self-explanatory village life had given place to a half blind struggle of individuals against circumstances and economic processes which no child could

possibly understand; and it was with the pitiful stock of ideas
to be derived from these conditions that the coal-carter passed
out of childhood, to enter upon the wage-earning career which
I have already outlined.

I need not spend much time in discussing that career as a
source of ideas. From first to last, and with the coal-carting
period thrown in, monotony rather than variety has been the
characteristic of it. I do not say that it has been quite fruitless.
There are impressions to be derived, and intense ones probably, from working all day against the "face" of a gravel-pit,
with the broken edge of the field up above one's head for
horizon; and from the skilled use of pick and shovel; and from
the weight of the wheelbarrow full of gravel as one wheels it
along a sagging plank. That is something to have experienced;
as it is to have sweated at night in a railway-cutting along with
other men under the eye of a ganger, and to have known
starlight, or rain, or frost, or fog, or tempest meanwhile. It is
something, even, to see the life of the roads year after year from
the footboard of a coal-van, and to be in charge of a horse hour
after hour; but I am talking now of ideas which might give
buoyancy and zest to the gossip beside a man's fireside in the
evening when he is tired; and I think it unnecessary to argue
that in regard to providing this kind of mental furniture, the
coal-carter's experience of life cannot have done great things
for him. It has been poverty-stricken just where the peasant
life was so rich; it has left a great deficiency, which could only
have been made good by an education intentionally given for
that end.

But it goes almost without saying that the man's "education" did very little to enrich his mind. The ideas and accomplishments he picked up at the elementary school between his
fourth and fourteenth years were of course in themselves insufficient for the needs of a grown man, and it would be unfair
to criticize his schooling from that standpoint. Its defect was
that it failed to initiate him into the inner significance of in-

formation in general, and failed wholly to start him on the path of learning. It was sterile of results. It opened to him no view, no vista; set up in his brain no stir of activity such as could continue after he had left school; and this for the reason that those simple items of knowledge which it conveyed to him were too scrappy and too few to begin running together into any understanding of the larger aspects of life. A few rules of arithmetic, a little of the geography of the British Islands, a selection of anecdotes from the annals of the ancient Jews; no English history, no fairy-tales or romance, no inkling of the infinities of time and space, or of the riches of human thought; but merely a few " pieces " of poetry, and a few haphazard and detached observations (called " Nature Study " nowadays) about familiar things—" the cat," " the cow," " the parsnip," " the rainbow," and so forth—this was the jumble of stuff offered to the child's mind—a jumble to which it would puzzle a philosopher to give coherence. And what could a child get from it to kindle his enthusiasm for that civilized learning in which, none the less, it all may have its place? When the boy left school his " education " had but barely begun.

And hardly anything has happened since then to carry it farther, although once there seemed just a chance of something better. During two successive winters the lad, being then from sixteen to seventeen years old, went to a night-school, which was opened for twenty-six weeks in each " session," and for four hours in each week. But the hope proved fallacious. In those hundred and four hours a year—hours which came after a tiring day's work—his brain was fed upon " mensuration " and " the science of horticulture," the former on the chance that some day he might want to measure a wall for paper-hanging or do some other job of the sort, and the latter in case fate should have marked him out for a nursery-gardener, when it would be handy to know that germinating seeds begin by pushing down a root and pushing up a leaf or two. This gives a notion of the sort of idea the luckless fellow derived from the night-school. I do not think that the joinery-classes at present being held in the night-school had begun in his time; but supposing that he also learnt joinery, he might, now that he is a man, add thoughts of mortices and tenons and mitre-joints to his other thoughts about wall areas and germinating seeds. Of course, all these things—like Jewish history or English geography—are worth knowing; but again it is true, of these things no less than of the childish learning acquired at the day-school, that whatever their worth may be to the people concerned to know them, they were very unlikely to set up in this young man's brain any constructive idea-activity, any refreshing form of thought that would enrich his leisure now, or give zest to his conversation. They were odds and ends of knowledge; more comparable to the numberless odds and ends in which peasants were so rich than to the flowing and luminous idea-life of modern civilization.

Adequate help having thus failed to reach the man from any source at any time of his life, it cannot be surprising if now the evening's opportunity finds him unprepared. He is between two civilizations, one of which has lapsed, while the other has not yet come his way. And what is true of him is true of the younger labouring men in general. In bread-and-cheese matters they are perhaps as well off as their forefathers in the village, but they are at a disadvantage in the matter of varied and successful vitality. The wage-earning thrift which has increased their usefulness as drudges has diminished their effectiveness as human beings; for it has failed to introduce into their homes those enlivening, those spirit-stirring influences which it denies to them when they are away from home doing their work. Hence a strange thing. The unemployed hours of the evening, which should be such a boon, are a time of blank and disconsolate tediousness, and when the longer days of the year come round many a man in the valley who ought to be glad of his spare time dodges the wearisome problem of what to do with it by putting himself to further work until he can go to bed without feeling that he has been wasting his life. Yet that is really no solution of the problem. It means that the men are trying to be peasants again, because they can discover no art of living, no civilization, compatible with the new thrift.

Of course it is true that they are handicapped by the lowness of the wages they receive. However much time one may have, it would be all but impossible to follow up modern civilization without any of its apparatus, in the shape of books and musical instruments, and the comfort of seclusion in a spare room; and none of these advantages can be bought out of an income of eighteen shillings a week. That is plainly the central difficulty —a difficulty which, unless it can be put right, condemns our commercial economy as wholly inadequate to the needs of labouring people. Supposing, however, that this defect could be suddenly remedied; supposing, that is, that by some miracle wages could be so adjusted as to put the labourer in command of the apparatus of civilization; still, he could not use the apparatus without a personal adjustment. He is impoverished, not in money only, but also in development of his natural faculties, since the old village civilization has ceased to help him.

XVII

THE WOMEN'S NEED

IF, while the common was still open, very few even of the men of the village troubled about regular employment, we may well believe that there were still fewer regular wage-earners amongst the women. I do not mean that wage-earning was a thing they never did. There was not a woman in the valley, perhaps, but had experience of it at hay-making and harvesting, while all would have been disappointed to miss the hop-picking. But these occasional employments had more resemblance to holidays and outings than they had to constant work for a living.

As the new thrift gradually established itself, the younger women at least had to alter their ways. For observe what had happened. A number of men, once half-independent, but now wanting work constantly, had been forced into a market where extra labour was hardly required; and it needs no argument to prove that, under such conditions, they were not only unable to command high wages, but were often unemployed. Of necessity, therefore, the women were obliged to make up the week's income by their own earnings. The situation, in fact, was similar to that which had been produced in earlier times and in other parishes by the old Poor Law, when parish pay enabled men to work for less than a living wage; only now the deficiency was made up, not at the expense of employers and ratepayers, but at the expense of women and girls.

But, though becoming wage-earners, the women missed the first advantage that wage-earners should enjoy—namely, leisure time. After all, the new thrift had but partially freed them from their old occupations. They might buy at a shop many things which their mothers had had to make; but there was no going to a shop to get the washing and scrubbing done, the beds made, the food cooked, the clothes mended. All this remained to the women as before. When they came home from the fields—at first it was principally by field-work that they earned wages—it was not to be at leisure, but to fall-to again on these domestic doings, just as if there had been no change, just as if they were peasant women still.

And yet, though this work had not changed, there was henceforth a vast difference in its meaning to the women. To approach it in the true peasant or cottage woman's temper was impossible; nor in doing it might the labourer's wife enjoy half the satisfaction that had rewarded the fatigue of her mother and grandmother. Something dropped away from it that could not be replaced when the old conditions died out.

To discover what the "something" was, one need not idealize those old conditions. It would be a mistake to suppose that the peasant economy, as practised in this valley, was nearly so good a thing for women as it was for the other sex; a mistake to think that their life was all honey, all simple sweetness and light, all an idyll of samplers and geraniums in cottage windows. On the contrary, I believe that very often it grew intensely ugly, and was as narrowing as it was ugly. The women saw nothing, and learnt nothing, of the outer world; and, in their own world, they saw and learnt much that was ill. All the brutalities connected with getting a living on peasant terms tended to coarsen them—the cruelties of men to one another, the horrors that had to be inflicted on animals, the miseries of disease suffered by ignorant human beings. Their perpetual attention to material cares tended to make them materialized and sordid; they grew callous; there was no room to cultivate delicacy of imagination. All this you must admit into the picture of the peasant woman's life, if you would try to see it fairly on the bad side as well as on the good side. Still, a good side there was, and that it was far oftener in evidence than the other I am well persuaded, when I remember the older village women who are dead now. They, so masculine in their outlook, yet so true-hearted and, now and then, so full of womanly tenderness and high feeling, could not have been the product of conditions that were often evil. And one merit in particular must be conceded to the old style of life. Say that the women's work was too incessant, and that some of it was distinctly ill to do; yet, taken as a whole, it was not uninteresting, and it was just that wholeness of it that made all the difference. The most tiresome duties—those domestic cares which were destined to become so irksome to women of a later day—were less tiresome because they were parts of a whole. Through them all shone the promise of happier hours to be won by their performance.

For although in this rough valley women might not achieve

the finer successes of cottage folk-life, where it led up into gracefulness and serenity, in a coarser fashion the essential spirit of pride in capable doing was certainly theirs. They could, and did, enjoy the satisfaction of proficiency, and win respect for it from their neighbours. If they were not neat, they were very handy; if there was no superlative finish about their work, there was soundness of quality, which they knew would be recognized as so much to their credit. Old gossip bears me out. Conceive the nimble and self-confident temper of those two cottage women—not in this village, I admit, but in the next one to it, and the thing was quite possible here—who always planned to do their washing on the same day, for the pleasure of seeing who had the most " pieces," and the best, to hang out on the clothes-lines. The story must be seventy years old, and I don't know who told it me; but it has always seemed to me very characteristic of the good side of cottage life, whether one thinks of the eager rivalry itself in the gardens, where the white clothes flapped, or of the long record implied in it of careful housewifery and quiet needlework. This spirit of joy in proficiency must have sweetened many of the cottage duties, and may well have run through them all. When a woman treated her friends to home-made wine at Christmas, she was exhibiting to them her own skill; when she cut up the loaf she had baked, or fried the bacon she had helped to cure, the good result was personal to herself; the very turf she piled on the fire had a homely satisfaction for her, because, cut as it was by her husband's own tools, and smelling of the neighbour-ing heath as it burnt, it was suggestive of the time-honoured economies of all the valley. In this way another comfort was added to that of her own more personal pleasure. For there was hardly a duty that the old-time village woman did, but was related closely to what the men were doing out of doors, and harmonized with the general industry of her people. She may be figured, almost, as the member of a tribe whose doings ex-plained all her own doings, and to whose immemorial customs her scrubbing and washing belonged, not unworthily. Her conscience was in the work. From one thing to another she went, now busily at a pleasant task, now doggedly at a wearisome one, and she knew no leisure; but at every point she was supported by what we may call the traditional feeling of the valley—nay, of the whole countryside—commending her perhaps; at any rate, fully understanding her position. To be like her mother and her grandmother; to practise the time-honoured habits, and to practise them efficiently, was a sort of religious cult with her, in the same way as it is nowadays with women of a certain position not to be dowdy. The peasant-cottager's wife could never think of herself as a mere charwoman or washerwoman; she had no such ignoble career. She was Mrs. This, or Dame That, with a recognized place in the village; and all the village traditions were her possession. The arts of her people—the flower-gardening, the songs and old sayings and superstitions, the customs of Harvest-time and Christmas— were hers as much as anybody's; if the stress of work kept her from partaking in them, still she was not shut out from them by reason of any social inferiority. And so we come back to the point at issue. House-drudgery might fill the peasant woman's days and years, and yet there was more belonging to it. It was the core of a fruit: the skeleton of something that was full of warm life. A larger existence wrapped it in, and on the whole a kindlier one.

In view of all this it is easy to see why the house-duties can no longer be approached in the old temper, or yield their former satisfaction while they are being done. The larger existence has been stripped away from them. They do not lead up to happier, more interesting, duties; they are not preparatory to pleasantness. The washing and scrubbing, the very cooking and needlework, are but so much trouble awaiting a woman when she gets up in the morning and when she comes home tired at night; they spoil the leisure that wage-earning should win, and they are undertaken, not with the idea of getting on to something productive, something that would make the cottage a more prosperous home, but solely to keep it from degenerating into an entirely offensive one. There is no hope surrounding these doings.

Nor do they fail only because they have become dissociated from pleasanter work. Even the best of them are actually less interesting in themselves. Look, for instance, at cooking. That cheap and coarse food which women now buy because its coarseness makes it cheap is of a quality to discourage any cook; it is common to the village—the rough rations of the poor; and the trumpery crocks and tins, the bad coal, and worse fire-places, do nothing to make the preparation of it more agreeable. With needlework it is the same story : commercial thrift has degraded that craft. She must be an enthusiast indeed who would expend any art of the needle upon the shabby second-hand garments, or the shoddy new ones, which have to content the labourer's wife. And if the family clothes are not good to make or to mend, neither are they good to wash, or worth displaying on the clothes-lines in the hope of exciting envy in neighbours.

Not at first, but in due time, inefficiency was added to the other causes which tended to make housework unpalatable to the women, and of no use to them as an uplifting experience. The inefficiency could hardly be avoided. The mothers, employed in the fields, had but little chance of teaching their daughters; and these daughters, growing up, to marry and to follow field-work themselves, kept their cottages as best they could, by the light of nature. In not a few cases all sense of an art of well-doing in such matters was lost, and the home became a place to sleep in, to feed in; not a place in which to try to live well. Perhaps the lowest ebb was reached some fifteen or twenty years ago. By then that feeling of belonging intimately to the countryside and sharing its traditions had died out, and nothing had come to replace it. For all practical purposes there were no traditions, nor were there any true country-folk living a peculiar and satisfying life of their own. The women had become merely the "hands" or employées of farmers, struggling to make up money enough every week for a wretched shopping. With health, a joking humour, and the inevitable habit of self-reliance, they preserved a careless good-temper, and they had not much time to realize their own plight; but it was, for all that, a squalid life that many of them led, a neglected life. Only in a very few cottages did their linger any serviceable memory of better things.

Of late years some recovery is discernible. Field-work, which fostered a blowsy carelessness, has declined, and at the same time the arrival of "residents" has greatly increased the demand for charwomen and washerwomen. The women, therefore, find it worth while to cultivate a certain tidiness in their persons, which extends to their homes. It is true I am told that their ideas of good housework are often rudimentary in the extreme; that the charwoman does not know when to change her scrubbing water; that the washerwoman is easily satisfied with quite dubious results; and I can well believe it. The state of the cottages is betrayed naïvely by the young girls who go from them into domestic service. "You don't seem to like things sticky," one of these girls observed to a mistress distressed by sticky door-handles one day and sticky table-knives the next day. That remark which Richard Jefferies heard a mother address to her daughter, "Gawd help the poor missus as gets hold o' *you*!" might very well be applied to many and many a child of fourteen in this valley, going out, all untrained, to her first "place"; but these things, indicating what has been and is, do not affect the truth that a slight recovery has occurred. It is an open question how much of the recovery is a revival of old ideas, called into play again by new forms of employment. Perhaps more of it is due to experience which the younger women now bring into the valley when they marry, after being in comfortable domestic service outside the valley. In other words, perhaps middle-class ideas of decent house-work are at last coming in, to fill the place left empty by the obsolete peasant ideas.

May we, then, conclude that the women are now in a fair way to do well; that nothing has been lost which those middle-class ideas cannot make good? In my view the circumstances warrant no such conclusion. Consider what it is that has to be made good. It is something in the nature of a civilization. It is the larger existence which enwrapped the peasant woman's house-drudgery and made it worth while. A good domestic method is all very well, and the middle-class method is probably better than the old method; but alike in the peasant cottages, and now in middle-class home, we may see in domestic work a nucleus only—the core of fruit, the necessary framework of a more acceptable life. With the cottage women in the old days that work favoured such developments of ability and of character as permitted the women to look with complacency upon women bred in other ways. They experienced no humiliating contrasts. Their household drudgery put within their reach the full civilization of which it was an organic part. But who can affirm as much of their household drudgery to-day? Who can pretend that the best accomplishment of it on middle-class lines admits the cottage woman into the full advantages of middle-class civilization, and enables her to look without humiliation upon the accomplishments of well-to-do women? I know that villa ladies and district visitors cling to some such belief, but the notion is false, and may be dismissed without argument, until the ladies can show that they owe all their own refinement to the inspiring influences of the washing-tub, and the scrubbing-pail, and the kitchen-range. The truth is that middle-class domesticity, instead of setting cottage women on the road to middle-class culture of mind and body, has side-tracked them—has made of them charwomen and laundresses, so that other women may shirk these duties and be "cultured."

Of course, their wage-earning and their home-work are not the only sources from which ideas that would explain and beautify life might be obtained from them. The other sources, however, are of no great value. At school, where (as we have seen) the boys get little enough general information, the girls have hitherto got less, instruction in needlework and cookery being given to them in preference to certain more bookish lessons that the boys get. They leave school, therefore, intellectually most ignorant. Then, in domestic service, again it is in cookery and that sort of thing that they are practised; there may be culture of thought and taste going on elsewhere in the house, but they are not admitted to it. Afterwards, marrying, and confronted with the problem of making both ends meet on eighteen shillings a week, they get experience indeed of many things, and, becoming mothers, they learn invaluable lessons; yet the *savoir vivre* that should make up for the old peasant cult, the happy outlook, the inspiring point of view, is not attained. Their best chance is in the ideas and knowledge they may pick up from their husbands, and if from them they do not learn anything of the best that has been thought and said in the world, they do not learn it. Of their husbands, in this connection, there will be something further to be said presently; in the meantime I may leave it to the reader to judge whether the cottage woman's needs, since the peasant system broke down, are being well met.

But I must not leave it to be inferred that the women, thus stranded between two civilizations, are therefore degraded or brutalized. From repeated experience one knows that their sense of courtesy—of good manners as distinct from merely fashionable or cultured manners—is very keen : in kindness and good-will they have nothing to learn from anybody, and most of their " superiors " and would-be teachers might learn from them. Nor would I disparage their improved house-keeping, as though it had no significance. It may open no doorway for them into middle-class civilization, but I think it

puts their spirits, as it were, on the watch for opportunities of
personal development. I judge by their looks. An expression,
not too often seen elsewhere, rests in the eyes of most of the
cottage women—an expression neither self-complacent nor de-
pressed, nor yet exactly docile, though it is near to that. The
interpretation one would put upon it depends on the phrases
one is wont to use. Thus some would say that the women
appear to be reaching out towards " respectability " instead of
the blowsy good-temper bred of field-work; others, more
simply, but perhaps more truly, that they are desirous of being
" good." But whatever epithet one gives it, there is the fine
look : a look hardly of expectancy—it is not alert enough for
that—but rather of patient quietness and self-possession, the
innermost spirit being held instinctively unsullied, in that re-
ceptive state in which a religion, a brave ethic, would flourish
if the seeds of such a thing could be sown there. A hopeful, a
generous and stimulating outlook—that is what must be re-
gained before the loss of the peasant outlook can be made good
to them. They are in want of a view of life that would re-
instate them in their own—yes, and in other people's—estima-
tion; a view of social well-being, not of the village only, but of
all England now, in which they can hold the position proper to
women who are wives and mothers.

And this, vague though it is, shows up some of the more
pressing needs of the moment. Above all things the economic
state of the cottage-women requires improvement. There must
be some definite leisure for them, and they must be freed from
the miserable struggle with imminent destitution, if they are
to find the time and the mental tranquillity for viewing life
largely. But leisure is not all. They need, further, an education to enable them to form an outlook fit for themselves; for
nobody else can provide them with such an outlook. The
middle-classes certainly are not qualified to be their teachers.
It may be said at once that the attempts of working-women
here and there to emulate women of the idle classes are of no

use to themselves and reflect small credit on those they imitate. In this connection some very curious things—the product of leisure and no outlook—are to be seen in the village. That objectionable yet funny cult of " superiority," upon which the " resident " ladies of the valley spend so much emotion, if not much thought, has its disciples in the cottages; and now and then the prosperous wife or daughter of some artisan or other gives herself airs, and does not " know," or will not " mix with," the wives and daughters of mere labourers in the neighbouring cottages. Whether women of this aspiring type find their reward, or mere bitterness, in the patronage of still higher women who are intimate with the clergy is more than I can say. The aspiration has nothing to do with that " religion," that new ethic, which I have just claimed to be the thing ultimately needed, before the loss of the peasant system can be made up to the women.

XVIII

THE WANT OF BOOK-LEARNING

SOME light was thrown on the more specific needs of the village by an experiment in which I had a share from ten to thirteen years ago. The absence of any reasonable pastime for the younger people suggested it. At night one saw boys and young men loafing and shivering under the lamp outside the public-house doors, or in the glimmer that shone across the road from the windows of the one or two village shops. They had nothing to do there but to stand where they could just see one another and try to be witty at one another's expense, or at the expense of any passers-by—especially of women—who might be considered safe game : that was their only way of spending the evenings and at the same time enjoying a little human companionship. True, the County Council had lately instituted evening classes for "technical education" in the elementary schools; but these classes were of no very attractive nature, and at best they occupied only two evenings a week. As many as twenty or five-and-twenty youths, however, attended them, glad of the warmth and light, though bored by the instruction. They were mischievous and inattentive; they kept close watch on the clock, and as soon as half-past nine came they were up and off helter-skelter, as if the gloomy precincts of the shop or the public-house were, after all, less irksome than the night-school.

There was no recreation whatever for the growing girls, none for the grown-up women; nothing but the public-house for the men, unless one excepts the two or three occasions during the winter when the more well-to-do residents chose to give an entertainment in the schoolroom, and admitted the poor into the cheaper seats. Everybody knows the nature of these functions. There were readings and recitations; young ladies sang drawing-room songs or played the violin; tableaux were displayed or a polite farce was performed; a complimentary speech wound up the entertainment; and then the performers withdrew again for several months into the aloofness of their residences, while the poor got through their winter evenings as best they could, in their mean cottages or under the lamp outside the public-house.

It was in full view of these circumstances that an "Entertainment Club" was started, with the idea of inducing the cottage people to help themselves in the matter of recreation instead of waiting until it should please others to come and amuse them. I am astonished now to think how democratic the club contrived to be. In the fortnightly programmes which were arranged the performers were almost exclusively of the wage-earning sort, and offers of help from "superior people" were firmly declined. And for at least one, and, I think, two winters, the experiment was wildly successful—so successful that, to the best of my recollection, the "gentry" were crowded out, and gave no entertainments at all. But the enthusiasm could not last. During the third winter decay set up, and early in the fourth the club, although with funds in hand, ceased its activities, leaving the field open, as it has since remained, to the recognized exponents of leisured culture.

The fact is, it died of their culture, or of a reflection of it. At the first nobody had cared a straw about artistic excellence. The homely or grotesque accomplishments of the village found their way surprisingly on to a public platform, and were not laughed to scorn; anyone who could sing a song or play a musical instrument—it mattered not what—was welcomed and applauded. But how could it go on? The people able to do anything at all were not many, and when their repertory of songs learnt by ear was exhausted, there was nothing new forthcoming. Gradually, therefore, the club began to depend on the few members with a smattering of middle-class attainments; and they, imitating the rich—asking for piano accompaniments to their singing, and so on—at the same time gave themselves airs of superiority to the crowd. And that was fatal. The less cultivated behaved in the manner usual to them where there is any unwarrantable condescension going—that is to say, they kept out of the way of it, until, finally, the performers and organizers had the club almost to themselves. From the outset the strong labouring men had contemptuously refused to have anything to do with what was often, I admit, a foolish and "gassy" affair; but their wives and sons and daughters had been very well pleased, until the taint of superiority drove them away. The club died when its democratic character was lost.

Yet, though I was glad to have done with it, I have never regretted the experience. It is easy now to see the absurdity of my idea, but at that time I knew less than I do now of the labouring people's condition, and in furthering the movement I entertained a shadowy hope of finding amongst the illiterate villagers some fragment or other of primitive art. It is almost superfluous to say that nothing of the sort was found. My neighbours had no arts of their own. For any refreshment of that kind they were dependent on the crumbs that fell from the rich man's table, or on such cheap refuse as had come into the village from London music-halls or from the canteens at Aldershot. Street pianos in the neighbouring town supplied them with popular airs, which they reproduced—it may be judged with what amazing effect—on flute or accordion; but the repertory of songs was filled chiefly from the sources just mentioned. The young men—the shyest creatures in the country, and the most sensitive to ridicule—found safety in comic songs which, if produced badly, raised but the greater laugh. Only once or twice were these songs imprudently chosen; as a rule, they dealt with somebody's misfortunes or discomforts, in a humorous, practical-joking spirit, and so came nearer, probably, to the expression of a genuine village sentiment than anything else that was done. But for all that they were an imported product. Instead of an indigenous folk-art, with its roots in the traditional village life, I found nothing but worthless forms of modern art which left the people's taste quite unfed. Once, it is true, a hint came that, democratic though the club might be, it was possibly not democratic enough. A youth mentioned that at home one evening he and his family had sat round the table singing songs, out of song-books, I think. It suggested that there might still lurk in the neglected cottages a form of artistic enjoyment more crude than anything that had come to light, and perhaps more native to the village. But I have no belief that it was so. Before I could inquire further, this boy dropped out of the movement. When asked why he had not come to one entertainment, he said that he had been sent off late in the afternoon to take two horses miles away down the country—I forget where—and had been on the road most of the night. A few weeks afterwards, turning eighteen, he went to Aldershot and enlisted. So far as I remember, he was the only boy of the true labouring class who ever took an active part in the proceedings—he performed once in a farce. The other lads, although some were sons of labourers and grandsons of peasants, were of those who had been apprenticed to trades, and therefore knew a little more than mere labourers, though I do not say that they were more intelligent by nature.

If, however, they were the pick of the village youth, the fact only makes the more impressive certain truths which forced themselves upon my notice at that time with regard to the needs of the village since the old peasant habits had vanished. There was no mistaking it : intercourse with these young men showed only too plainly how slow modern civilization had been to follow modern methods of industry and thrift. Understand, they were well-intentioned and enterprising fellows. They had begun to look beyond the bounds of this parish, and to seek for adaptations to the larger world. Moreover, they were learning trades—those very trades which have since been introduced into our elementary schools as a means of quickening the children's intellectual powers. But these youths somehow had not drawn enlightenment from their trades, being, in fact, handicapped all the time by the want of quite a different education. To put it rather brutally, they did not understand their own language— the standard English language in which modern thinking has to go on in this country.

For several of the entertainments they came forward to perform farces. After the first diffidence had worn off, they took a keen delight in the preparations, working hard and cordially; they were singularly ready to be shown what to do, and to be criticized. " Knock-about " farce—the counterpart in drama of their comic songs—pleased them best, and they did well in it. But *Box and Cox* was almost beyond them, because they missed the meanings of the rather stilted dialogue. In helping to coach them in their parts I had the best of opportunities to know this. They produced a resemblance to the sound of the sentences, and were satisfied, though they missed the sense.

Instead of saying that he " divested " himself of his clothing, Mr. Box—or was it Cox?—said that he " invested " himself, and no correction could cure him of saying that. When one of them came to describing the lady's desperate wooing of him, " to escape her importunities " is what he should have said; but what he did say was " to escape our opportunities "—an error which the audience, fortunately, failed to notice, for it slipped out again at the time of performance, after having been repeatedly put right at rehearsal. And this sort of thing happened all through the piece. Almost invariably the points which depended on a turn of phrase were lost. " I at once give you warning that I give you warning at once " became, " I at once give you warning. That is, I give you warning at once." Cox (or Box) reading the lawyer's letter, never made out the following passage : " I soon discovered her will, the following extract from which will, I am sure, give you satisfaction." It was plain that he thought the second word " will " meant the same as the first.

As evidence of a lack of " book-learning " in the village, this might have been insufficient, had it stood alone. But it did not. The misbehaviour of the boys at the night-school has been mentioned. Being a member of the school managing committee, I went to the school occasionally, and what I saw left me satisfied that a large part of the master's difficulty arose from the unfamiliarity of the scholars with their own language. That initial ignorance blocked the road to science even more completely than, in the Entertainment Club, it did to art. " The Science of Horticulture " was the subject of the lesson on one dismal evening, this being the likeliest of some half-dozen " practical sciences " prescribed for village choice by the educational authority at Whitehall. About twenty " students," ranging from sixteen to nineteen years old, were—no, not puzzling over it : they were " putting in time " as perfunctorily as they dared, making the lesson an excuse for being present together in a warmed and lighted room. When I went in it was near the close of the evening; new matter was being entered upon, apparently as an introduction to the next week's lesson. I stood and watched. The master called upon first one, then another, to read aloud a sentence or two out of the textbook with which each was provided; and one after another the boys stood up, shamefaced or dogged, to stumble through sentences which seemed to convey absolutely no meaning to them. If it had been only the hard words that floored them—such as "cotyledon" and "dicotyledon"—I should not have been surprised; but they blundered over the ordinary English, and had next to no sense of the meaning of punctuation. I admit that probably they were not trying to do their best; that they might have put on a little intentional clumsiness, in the instinctive hope of escaping derision by being thought waggish. But the pity of it was that they should need to protect themselves so. They had not the rudimentary accomplishment : that was the plain truth. They could not understand ordinary printed English.

Of science, of course, they were learning nothing. They may have taken away from those lessons a few elementary scientific terms, and possibly they got hold of the idea of the existence of some mysterious knowledge that was not known in the village; but the advantage ended there. I doubt if a single member of the class had begun to use his brain in a scientific way, reasoning from cause to effect; I doubt if it dawned upon one of them that there was such an unheard-of accomplishment to be acquired. They were trying—if they were trying anything at all—to pick up modern science in the folk manner, by rote, as though it were a thing to be handed down by tradition. So at least I infer, not only from watching this particular class then and on other occasions, but also from the following circumstance.

At Christmastime in one of these winters a few of the boys of the night-school went round the village, mumming. They performed the same old piece that Mr. Hardy has described in

The Return of the Native—the same old piece that, as a little child, I witnessed years ago in a real village; but it had degenerated lamentably. The boys said that they had learnt it from an elder brother of one of them, and had practised it in a shed; and at my request the leader consented to write out the piece, and in due time he brought me his copy. I have mislaid the thing, and write from memory; but I recall enough of it to affirm that he had never understood, or even cared to fix a meaning to, the words—or sounds, rather—which he and his companions had gabbled through as they prowled around the kitchen clashing their wooden swords. That St. George had become King William was natural enough; but what is to be said of changing the Turkish Knight into the Turkish Snipe? That was one of the " howlers " this youth perpetrated, amongst many others less striking, perhaps, but not less instructive. The whole thing showed plainly where the difficulty lay at the night-school. The breaking up of the traditional life of the village had failed to supply the boys either with the language or with the mental habits necessary for living successfully under the new conditions. Some of these boys were probably the sons of parents unable to read and write; none of them came from families where those accomplishments were habitually practised or much esteemed.

The argument, thus illustrated by the state of the boys, extends in its application to practically the whole of the village. " Book-learning " had been very unimportant to the peasant with his traditional lore, but it would be hard to exaggerate the handicap against which the modern labourer strives, for want of it. Look once more at his position. In the new circumstance the man lives in an environment never dreamt of by the peasant. Economic influences affecting him most closely come, as it were, vibrating upon him from across the sea. Vast commercial and social movements, unfelt in the valley under the old system, are altering all its character; instead of being one of a group of villagers tolerably independent of the rest of the world, he is entangled in a network of economic forces as wide as the nation; and yet, to hold his own in this new environment, he has no new guidance. Parochial customs and the traditions of the village make up the chief part of his equipment.

But for national intercourse parochial customs and traditions are almost worse than none at all—like a Babel of Tongues. National standards have to be set up. We cannot, for instance, deal in Winchester quarts and Cheshire acres, in long hundreds and baker's dozens; we have no use for weights and measures that vary from county to county, or for a token coinage that is only valid in one town or one trade. But most of all, for making our modern arrangements a standard English language is so necessary that those who are unfamiliar with it can neither manage their own affairs efficiently nor take their proper share in the national life.

And this is the situation of the labourer to-day. The weakness of it, moreover, is in almost daily evidence. One would have thought that at least in a man's own parish and his own private concerns illiteracy would be no disadvantage; yet, in fact, it hampers him on every side. Whether he would join a benefit society, or obtain poor-law relief, or insure the lives of his children, or bury his dead, or take up a small holding, he finds that he must follow a nationalized or standardized procedure, set forth in language which his forefathers never heard spoken and never learned to read. Even in the things that are really of the village the same conditions prevail. The slate-club is managed upon lines as businesslike as those of the national benefit society. The "Institute" has its secretary, and treasurer, and balance-sheet, and printed rules; the very cricket club is controlled by resolutions proposed and seconded at formal committee meetings, and duly entered in minute-books. But all this is a new thing in the village, and no guidance for it is to be found in the lingering peasant traditions.

To this day, therefore, the majority of my neighbours, whose ability for the work they have been prepared to do proves them

to be no fools, are, nevertheless, pitiably helpless in the management of their own affairs. Most disheartening it is, too, for
those whose help they seek, to work with them. In the cricket-
club committee, on which I served for a year or two, it was
noticeable that the members, eager for proper arrangements to
be made, often sat tongue-tied and glum, incapable of urging
their views, so that only after the meeting had broken up and
they had begun talking with one another did one learn that the
resolutions which had been passed were not to their mind.
Formalities puzzled them—seemed to strike them as futilities.
And so in other matters besides cricket. A local builder—a
man of blameless integrity—had a curious experience. Some-
what against his wishes, he was appointed treasurer of the
village Lodge of Oddfellows; but when, inheriting a considerable sum of money, he began to buy land and build houses,
nothing would persuade the illiterate members of the society
that he was not speculating with their funds. Audited accounts
had no meaning for them; possibly the fact that he was doing a
service for no pay struck them as suspicious; at any rate they
murmured so openly that he threw up his office. Whom they
have got in his place, and whether they are suspicious of him
too, I do not know. My point is that, while modern thrift
obliges them to enter into these fellowships, they remain, for
mere want of book-learning, unable to help themselves, and
dependent on the aid of friends from the middle or employing
classes. In other words, the greater number of the Englishmen
in the village have to stand aside and see their own affairs controlled for them by outsiders.

This is so wholly the case in some matters that nobody ever
dreams of consulting the people who are chiefly concerned in
them. In the education of their children, for one thing, they
have no voice at all. It is administered in a standardized form
by a committee of middle-class people appointed in the neighbouring town, who carry out provisions which originate from
unapproachable permanent officials at Whitehall. The County

Council may modify the programme a little; His Majesty's inspectors—strangers to the people, and ignorant of their needs —issue fiats in the form of advice to the school teachers; and meanwhile the parents of the children acquiesce, not always approving what is done, but accepting it as if it were a law of fate that all things must be arranged over their heads by the classes who have book-learning.

And this customary attitude of waiting for what the " educated " may do for them renders them apathetic where they might be, and where it is highly important that they should be, reliant upon their own initiative—I mean, in political action. The majority of the labourers in the village have extremely crude ideas of representative government. A candidate for Parliament is not, in their eyes, a servant whom they may appoint to give voice to their own wishes; he is a " gentleman " who, probably from motives of self-interest, comes to them as a sort of quack doctor, with occult remedies, which they may have if they will vote for him, and which might possibly do them good. Hence they hardly look upon the Government as an instrument at all under the control of people like themselves; they view it, rather, as a sort of benevolent tyranny, whose constitution is no concern of theirs. Commons or Lords, Liberals or Tories—what does it matter to the labourer which of them has the power, so long as one or other will cast an occasional look in his direction, and try to do something or other to help him? What they should do rests with the politicians : it is their part to suggest, the labourer's to acquiesce.

Such are some of the more obvious disabilities from which the cottage people suffer, largely for want of book-learning. I think, however, that they are beginning to be aware of the disadvantage, for, though they say little about it, I have heard of several men getting their children to teach them, in the evening, the lessons learnt at school during the day. Certainly the old contempt for " book-learning " is dying out. And now and then one hears the most ingenuous confessions of incompetence to understand matters of admitted interest. An old woman, discussing "Tariff Reform," said : "We sort o' people can't understand it for ourselves. What we wants is for somebody to come and explain it to us. And then," she added, "we dunno whether we dares believe what they says." If you could hear one even of the better-taught labourers trying to read out something from a newspaper, you would appreciate his difficulties. He goes too slowly to get the sense; the end of a paragraph is too far from the beginning of it; the thread of the argument is lost sight of. An allusion, a metaphor, a parenthesis, may easily make nonsense of the whole thing to a reader who has never heard of the subject alluded to, or of the images called up by the metaphor, and whose mind is unaccustomed to those actions of pausing circumspection which a parenthesis demands.

XIX

EMOTIONAL STARVATION

REMEMBERING the tales which get into the papers now and then of riot amongst the "high-spirited young gentlemen" at the Universities, I am a little unwilling to say more about the unruliness of our village youths, as though it were something peculiar to their rank of life. Yet it must not be quite passed over. To be sure, not all the village lads, any more than all undergraduates, are turbulent and mischievous; and yet here, as at Oxford, there is a minority who apparently think it manly to be insubordinate and to give trouble, while here, just as there, the better sense of the majority is too feeble to make up a public opinion which the offenders would be afraid to defy. The disorder of the village lads was noticeable long ago at the night-school; for example, on an evening shortly after the "Khaki" election, when Mr. Brodrick (now Lord Midleton) had been re-elected for this division. On that evening a lecture on Norway, illustrated by lantern slides, could hardly be got through owing to the liveliness of a few lads, who amused all their comrades by letting off volleys of electioneering cries. I have forgotten who the lecturer was, but I remember well how the shouts of " Good old Brodrick!" often prevailed, so that one could not hear the man's voice. Since then there have been more striking examples of the same sort of vivacity. Not two winters ago the weekly meetings of a " boys' club," which aimed only to help the village lads pass an evening sensibly, had to be abandoned, owing to the impossible behaviour of the members. One week I heard that they had run amok amongst the furniture of the schoolroom where the meetings were held; on the next, they blew out the lamps, and locked one of the organizers into the room for an hour; and a week or two afterwards they piled window-curtains and door-mats on to the fire, and nearly got the building ablaze. In short, to judge from what was told me, there seems to have been little to distinguish them from frolicsome undergraduates, save their poverty-stricken clothes and their unaspirated speech. It is true they kept their excesses within doors, but then, they had no influential relatives to take their part against an interfering police force; and moveover, most of them came to the meetings a little subdued by ten hours or so of work at wage-earning. Still, their "high spirits" were in evidence, uncontrolled—just as elsewhere—by any high sentiment. The sense of personal responsibility for their actions, the power to understand that there is such a thing as " playing the game " even towards people in authority or towards the general public, seemed to be as foreign to them as if they had never had to soil their hands with hard work.

Whatever may be the case with others, in the village lads a merely intellectual unpreparedness is doubtless partly accountable for this behaviour. The villagers having had no previous experience of action in groups, unless under compulsion like that of the railway-ganger or of the schoolmaster with his cane, it is strange now to the boys to find themselves at a school where there is no compulsion, but all is left to their voluntary effort. And stranger still is the club. A formal society, dependent wholly on the loyal co-operation of its members and yet enforcing no obvious discipline upon them, is a novelty in village life. The idea of it is an abstraction, and because the old-fashioned half-peasant people fifty years ago never needed to think about abstractions at all, it turns out now that no family habit of mind for grasping such ideas has come down from them to their grandsons.

This mental inefficiency, however, is only a form—a definite form for once—of a more vague but more prevalent backwardness. The fact is that the old ideas of conduct in general are altogether too restricted for the new requirements, so that the village life suffers throughout from a sort of ethical starvation. I gladly admit that, for the day's work and its hardships, the surviving sentiments in favour of industry, patience, good-humour, and so on, still are strong; and I do not forget the admirable spirit of the cottage women in particular; yet it is true that for the wider experiences of modern life other sentiments or ideals, in addition to those of the peasants, need development, and that progress in them is behindhand in the village. What the misbehaviour of the village boys illustrates in one direction may be seen in other directions amongst the men and women and children.

Like other people, the cottagers have their emotional susceptibilities, which, however, are either more robust than other people's or else more sluggish. At any rate it takes more than a little to disturb them. During last winter I heard of a man—certainly he was one of the older sort, good at many an obsolete rural craft—who had had chilblains burst on his fingers, and had sewn up the wounds himself with needle and cotton. There is no suspicion of inhumanity against him, yet it seemed to me that in fiercer times he would have made a willing tor-

turer; and other little incidents—all of them recent ones too—
came back to my mind when I heard of him. In one of these
a servant-girl from the village was concerned—a quiet and
timid girl she was said to be; yet, on her own initiative, and
without consulting her mistress, she drowned a stray cat which
was trying to get a footing in the household. Again, I myself
heard and wondered at the happy prattle of two little girls—
the children, they, of a most conscientious man and woman—
as they told of the fun they had enjoyed, along with their
father and mother, in watching a dog worry a hedgehog. And
yet it is plain enough that the faculty for compassion and kindness is inborn in the villagers, so that their susceptibilities
might just as well be keen as blunt. In their behaviour to their
pets the gentle hands and the caressing voices betoken a great
natural aptitude for tenderness. And not to their pets only.
All one afternoon I heard, proceeding from a pig-stye, the voice
of an elderly man who was watching an ailing sow there.
"*Come* on, ol' gal . . . *come* on, ol' gal," he said, over and
over again in tireless repetition, as sympathetically as if he were
talking to a child. Where the people fail in sensitiveness is
from a want of imagination, as we say, though we should say,
rather, a want of suppleness in their ideas. They can sympa-
thize when their own dog or cat is suffering, because use has
wakened up their powers in that direction; but they do not
abstract the idea of suffering life and apply it to the tormented
hedgehog, because their ideas have not been practised upon
imagined or non-existent things in such a way as to become, as
it were, a detached power of understanding, generally applic-
able.

But is it to be wondered at if some unlovely features appear
in the village character? Or is it not rather a circumstance to
give one pause, that these commercially unsuccessful and
socially neglected people, whose large families the self-satisfied
eugenist views with such solemn misgivings, should be in the

main so kindly, so generous, and sometimes so lofty in their sentiments as in fact they are? With like disadvantages, where are there any other people in the country who would do so bravely? If it is clear that they miss a rich development of their susceptibilities, a reason why is no less clear. I have just hinted at it. The ample explanation is in the fact that they have hardly any imaginary or non-existent subjects upon which to exercise emotional sensibility for its own sake, so that it may grow strong and fine by frequent practice; but they have to wait for some real thing to move them—some distressful occurrence in the valley itself, like that mentioned earlier in this book, when a man trimming a hedge all but killed his own child, and a thrill of horror shuddered through the cottages. Of matters like this the people talk with an excited fascination, there being so little else to stir them. Instead of the moving accident by flood or field, they have the squalid or merely agonizing accident. Sickness amongst friends or neighbours affords another topic upon which their emotion seeks exercise: they linger over the discussion of it, talking in moaning tones instinctively intended to stimulate feeling. Then there are police-court cases. Some man gets drunk, and is fined; or cannot pay his rent, and is turned out of his cottage; or misbehaves in such a way that he is sent to gaol. The talk of it threads its swift way about the village—goes into intimate details, too, relating how the culprit's wife "took on" when her man was sentenced; or how his children suffer; or perhaps how the magistrates bullied him, or how he insulted the prosecuting lawyer.

It is natural that the people should be greedy readers (when they can read at all) of the sensational matter supplied by newspapers. Earthquakes, railway disasters, floods, hurricanes, excite them not really disagreeably. So, too, does it animate them to hear of prodigies and freaks of Nature, as when, a little while ago, the papers told of a man whose flesh turned "like marble," so that he could not bend his limbs for fear lest they should snap. Anything to wonder at will serve; anything about which they can exclaim. That feeling of the crowd when fireworks call forth the fervent " O-oh!" of admiration, is the village feeling which delights in portents of whatever kind. But nothing else is quite so effectual to that end as are crimes of violence, and especially murder. For, after all, it is the human element that counts; and these descendants of peasants, having no fictitious means of acquainting themselves with human passion and sentiment, such as novels and dramas supply in such abundance to other people, turn with all the more avidity to the unchosen and unprepared food furnished to their starving faculties by contemporary crime.

There is, indeed, another side to their sensationalism which should be noticed. I was a little startled some years ago by a scrap of conversation between two women. The papers at that time were full of a murder which had been committed in a village neighbouring this, the young man accused of it being even then on his trial. It was in the evidence that he had visited his home quite an hour after the time when the deed must have been done, and these women were discussing that point, one of them saying : " I don't believe *my* boy would ha' come 'ome that Sunday night if *he'd* ha' done it." It was surprising to me to hear a respectable mother speculate as to how her own son would behave in such a case, or contemplate even the possibility of his being guilty of murder; and I thought it all too practical a way of considering the subject. But it revealed how appallingly real such things may be to people who, as I tried to show farther back, have reason to feel a little like an alien race under our middle-class law. Very often one may discern this personal or practical point of view in their sensationalism : they indulge it chiefly for the sake of excitement, but with a side glance at the bearing which the issue may have upon their own affairs. In a foul case which was dealt with under the Criminal Law Amendment Act, large numbers of our cottage women flocked to the town to hear the trial, attracted partly by the hope of sensation, of course, but also very largely actuated by a sentiment of revenge against the offender; for here the safety of their own young daughters was involved.

Be this as it may, still it is true that the two sources I have mentioned—namely, the sensational news in the papers and the distresses and misdemeanours in the village itself—supply practically all that the average cottager gets to touch his sentiments and emotions into life; and it is plain enough that from neither of these sources, even when supplemented by a fine traditional family life, can a very desirable spiritual nourishment be obtained. " Real " enough the fare is, in all conscience; but, as usual with realities of that sort, it wants choiceness. It provides plenty of objects for compassion, for anxiety, for contempt, for ridicule even, but very little for emulation, for reverence. The sentiments of admiration and chivalry, the enthusiastic emotions, are hardly ever aroused in man or woman, boy or girl, in the village. Nothing occurs in the natural course to bring what is called " good form " into notice and make it attractive, and at the same time the means of bringing this about by art demand more money, more leisure and seclusion, more book-learning too, than the average labourer can obtain. In the middle-classes this is not the case. It is true that the middle-classes have little to boast of in this respect, but generous ideas of modesty and reverence, and of " playing the game " and of public duty, and of respect for womanhood, have at least a chance of spreading amongst boys and girls, in households where art and books are valued, and where other things are talked of than the sordid scandals of the valley and of the police-courts. The difference that the want of this help may make was brought forcibly home to me one day. I came upon a group of village boys at play in the road, just as one of them—a fellow about thirteen years old—conceived a bright idea for a new game. " Now I'll be a murderer!" he cried, waving his arms ferociously.

There are other circumstances that tend to keep the standard of sentiment low. As the boys begin to work for money at so early an age, the money-value of conduct impresses itself strongly upon them, and they soon learn to think more of what they can get than of what they can do or are worth. And while they have lost all the steadying influence that used to flow from the old peasant crafts, they get none of the steadiness which would come from continuity of employment. The work they do as errand-boys calls neither for skill in which they might take pride nor for constancy to any one master; but it encourages them to be mannish and " knowing " long before their time. Of course the more generous sentiments are at a discount under such conditions.

Then, too, there can be little doubt that the " superior " attitude of the employing classes has its injurious effect upon the village character. The youth who sees his father and mother and sisters treated as inferiors, and finds that he is treated so too, is led unconsciously to take a low view of what is due either to himself or to his friends. The sort of view he takes may be seen in his behaviour. The gangs of boys who troop and lounge about the roads on Sundays are generally being merely silly in the endeavour to be witty. They laugh loudly, yet not humorously and kindly (one very rarely hears really jolly laughter in the village), but in derision of one another or of the wayfarers—girls by preference. So far as one can overhear it, their fun is always of that contumacious character, and it must be deadly to any sentiment of modesty, or honour, or reverence.

It requires but little penetration to see how these circumstances react upon the village girls. The frolicsome and giddy appear to enjoy themselves as much as the boys do, but the position must be cruel to those of a serious tendency. To be treated with disrespect and be made the subjects of rough wit as they go about is only the more acute part of their difficulty. One may suppose that at home they find little appreciation of any high sentiments, but are driven, in self-defence, to be rather flippant, rather "worldly." The greater number of house mistresses, meanwhile, if one may judge from their own complacent conversation, behave in a way most unlikely to contribute to their servants' self-respect. It is hard to believe that any really high sentiment is to be learnt from women who, for all the world as if they were village louts, make light of a girl's feelings, and regard her love-affairs especially as a proper subject for ridicule or for suspicion.

XX

THE CHILDREN'S NEED

As one of the managing committee of the village schools for a good many years, I have had considerable opportunity of watching the children collectively. The circumstances, perhaps, are not altogether favourable to the formation of trustworthy opinions. Seen in large numbers, and under discipline too, the children look too much alike; one misses the infinite variety of their personalities such as would appear in them at home. On the other hand, characteristics common to them all, which might pass unnoticed in individuals, become obvious enough when there are many children together.

In the main the " stock " has always seemed to me good, and to some extent my impression is supported by the results of the medical inspection now undertaken at the schools by the County Council. Such defects as the doctor finds are generally of no deep-seated kind : bad teeth, faulty vision (often due, probably, to improper use of the eyes in school), scalp troubles, running ears, adenoids, and so on, are the commonest. Insufficient nutrition is occasionally reported. In fact the medical evidence tells, in a varied form, much the same tale that school managers have been able to read for themselves in the children's dilapidated boots and clothes, and their grimy hands and uncared-for hair, for it all indicates poverty at home, want of convenience for decent living, and ignorance as well as carelessness in the parents. All this we have known, but now we learn from the doctor that the evil effects of these causes do not stop at the clothes and skin, but go a little deeper. Yet probably they have not hurt the essential nature of the children. Congenital defects are rare; the doctor discovers even a high average of constitutional fitness, due, it may be, to severe " natural " selection weeding out the more delicate. It is certain that the village produces quite a fair proportion of really handsome children, besides those of several of the old families, who are wont to be of exceptional beauty. Unhappily, before the school-years are over, the fineness usually begins to disappear, being spoilt, I suspect, partly by the privations of the home-life and partly by another cause, of which I will speak by-and-by.

I think, further—but it is only a vague impression, not worth much attention—that as regards physique the girls are as a rule more thriving and comely than the boys. The latter appear very apt to become knotted and hard, and there is a want of generosity in their growth, as though they received less care than the girls, and were more used to going hungry and being cold and wet. But if my impression is right, there are two points to be noticed in further explanation of it. The first point relates to the early age at which the boys begin to be useful at work. It has been already told how soon they are set to earn a little money out of school-hours; but even before that stage is reached the little boys have to make themselves handy. On the Saturday holiday it is no uncommon thing to see a boy of eight or nine pushing up the hill a little truck loaded with coal or coke, which he has been sent to buy at the railway yard. Smaller ones still are sent to the shops, and not seldom they are really overloaded. Thus at an age when boys in better circumstances are hardly allowed out alone, these village children practise perforce a considerable self-reliance, and become acquainted with the fatigue of labour. Some little chaps, as they go about their duties—leading lesser brothers by the hand perhaps, or perhaps dealing very sternly with them, and making them "keep up" without help—have unawares the manner of responsible men.

That is one point which may help to account for the apparent physical disparity between the boys and girls of the village. The other is the subject of a remark amongst all who know the school-children. There is no doubt about it; whether the girls are comelier of growth than the boys or not, they are in behaviour so much more civilized than one might almost suppose them to come from different homes. To my mind this might be sufficiently explained by the fact that they are usually spared those burdensome errands and responsibilities which are thrust so soon upon their brothers; but the schoolmaster has another explanation, which probably contains some truth. His view is that at home the girls come chiefly under the influence of their mothers, whose experience of domestic service gives them an idea of manners, while the boys take pattern from their fathers, whose work encourages roughness. Whatever the cause, the fact remains : the boys may be physically as sound as the girls, but they certainly have less charm. It is not often delightful to see them. They do not stand up well; they walk in a slouching and narrow-chested way; and, though they are mischievous enough, there is strangely wanting in them an air of alertness, of vivacity, of delight in life. There is no doubt that their heavily-ironed and ill-fitting boots cause them to walk badly; yet it is only reasonable to suppose that this is but one amongst many difficulties, and that, in general, the conditions in which the boys live are unfavourable to a good physical growth.

As regards intellectual power, in boys and girls too, the evidence—to be quite frank—does not bear out all that I wish to believe; for, in spite of appearances, I am not yet persuaded that these cottage children are by birth more dull of wit than town-bred children and those in better circumstances. It must be remembered that in this village, so near as it is to a town, there has been little of that migration to towns which is said to have depleted other villages of their cleverer people. A few lads go to sea, more than a few into the army; some of the girls marry outside, and are lost to the parish. But it would be easy to go through the valley and find, in cottage after cottage, the numerous descendants of old families that flourished here, and were certainly not deficient in natural brain-power, two generations ago, although it was not developed in them on modern lines. Nor need one go back two generations. To be acquainted with the fathers and mothers of the school-children is to know people whose minds are good enough by nature, and are only wanting in acquired power; and when, aware of this, one goes into the school and sees the children of these parents, some of them very graceful, with well-shaped heads and eyes that can sparkle and lips that can break into handsome, laughing curves, it is very hard to believe that the breed is dull. The stupidity is more likely due merely to imperfect nurture; at any rate, one should not accept an explanation of it that disparages the village capacity for intelligence until it is made clear that the state of the children cannot be explained in any other way.

Leaving explanations aside, however, there is the fact, not to be gainsaid, that the children in general are slow of wit. One notes it in the infant school first, and especially in the very youngest classes. There, newly come from their mother's care the small boys and girls from five to six years old have often a wonderfully vacant expression. There is little of that speculative dancing of the eyes, that evident appetite for perceptions and ideas, which you will find in well-to-do nurseries and play-rooms. And whereas in the latter circumstances children will take up pencil or paintbrush confidently, as if born to master those tools, the village infant is hesitating, clumsy, feeble. Upon the removal of a child to the upper or "mixed" school, a certain increase of intelligence often seems to come at a bound. The circumstance is highly suggestive. The " infant " of seven is suddenly brought into contact with older scholars already familiarized with particular groups of ideas, and those ideas are speedily absorbed by the little ones, while the swifter methods of teaching also have their quickening effect, for a time. But after this jump has been made and lost sight of—that is to say amongst the older scholars, who do not again meet with such a marked change of environment—one is again aware of considerable mental density throughout the school. The children resemble their parents. They are quick enough to observe details, though not always the details with which the teacher is concerned, but they have very little power of dealing with the simplest abstractions. They are clumsy in putting two thoughts together for comparison; clumsy in following reasons, or in discussing underlying principles. In short, " thinking " is an art they hardly begin to practise. They can learn and apply a " rule of thumb," a folk-rule, so to speak—but there is no flow, nor anything truly consecutive, in the movement of their ideas. Elsewhere one may hear children of six or seven—little well-cared-for people—keep up a continual stream of intelligent and happy talk with their parents or nursemaids; but to the best of my belief this does not happen amongst the village children, at any age.

Observations of them at play, in the cottage gardens or on the road, throw some light on their condition. It would appear that they are extremely ill-supplied with subjects to think about. In the exercise of imagination, other children fall naturally into habits of consecutive thought, or at any rate of consecutive fancy; but these of the labouring class have hardly any ideas which their young brains could play with, other than those derived from their own experience of real life in the valley, or those which they hear spoken of at home. Hence in their histrionic games of " pretending " it is but a very limited repertory of parts that they can take. Two or three times I have come upon a little group of them under a hedgerow or sun-warmed bank, playing at school; the teacher being delightfully severe, and the scholars delightfully naughty. And now and again there is a feeble attempt at playing soldiers. Very often, too, one may see boys, in string harness, happy in being very mettle-some horses. In one case a subtle variant of this game inspired two small urchins to what was, perhaps, as good an imagina-tive effort as I have met with in the village. The horse, instead of being frisky, was being slow, so that the driver had to swear at him. And most vindictive and raucous was the infant voice that I heard saying, " Git up, you blasted lazy cart-'orse!" Other animals are sometimes represented. With a realistic grunt, a little boy, beaming all over his face, said to his com-panion, " Now I'll be your pig." Another day it puzzled me to guess what a youngster was doing as he capered furiously about the road, wearing his cap pushed back and two short sticks protruding from beneath it over his forehead; but presently I perceived that he was a " bullick " being driven to market. Excepting the case already mentioned, of the boy who proposed to " be a murderer," I do not recall witnessing any other forms of the game of " pretending " amongst the village children, unless in the play of little girls with their dolls. There was one very pretty child who used to prattle to me sometimes about her " baby," and how it had been " bad," that is to say, naughty, and put to bed; or had not had its break-fast. This little girl was an orphan who lived with her grand-father and a middle-aged aunt, and was much petted by them. She was almost alone too, amongst the village children of that period, in being the possessor of a doll, for no more than five or six years ago one rarely saw such a thing in the village. Christmas-trees have since done something to make up the deficiency. A month or two ago I saw a four-year-old girl—a friend of mine from a neighbour's cottage—solemnly walking down a by-lane alone, carrying a rag-doll half as big as herself. I stopped, and admired; but, in spite of her pride, she took a

very matter-of-fact view of her toy. " It's head keeps comin'
off," was all that she could be persuaded to say.

" Matter-of-fact " is what the children are, for the most part.
One autumn evening, after dark, tittering and little squeals of
excitement sounded from a neighbour's garden, where a man,
going to draw water from his well, and carrying a lantern, was
accompanied by four or five children. In the security of his
presence they were pretending to be afraid of "bogies." " If a
bogie was to come," I heard, " I should get up that apple-tree,
and then if he come up after me I should get down t'other
side." An excited laugh was followed by the man's contemptuous remonstrance, " *Shut* up!" which produced silence
for a minute or two, until the party were returning to the
cottage; when a very endearing voice called softly, " Bo-gie!
Bo-gie! Come, bogie!" This instance of fancy in a cottage
child stands, however, alone in my experience. I have never
heard anything else like it in the village. The children romp
and squabble and make much noise; they play, though rarely,
at hide-and-seek; or else they gambol about aimlessly, or try to
sing together, or troop off to look at the fowls or the rabbits.
The bigger children are as a rule extremely kind to the lesser
ones. A family of small brothers and sisters who lived near me
some time ago were most pleasant to listen to for this reason.
The smallest of them, a three-year-old boy commonly called
" 'Arry," was their pet. " Look, 'Arry; here's a *dear* little
flow-wer! A little 'arts-ease—look, 'Arry!" " 'Ere, 'Arry,
have a bite o' this nice apple!" They were certainly attractive
children, though formidably grubby as to their faces. I heard
them with their father, admiring a litter of young rabbits in
the hutch. " O-oh, en't that a *dear* little thing!" they ex-
claimed, again and again. Sunday was especially delightful to
them because their father was at home then; and I liked to
hear him playing with them. One particularly happy hour
they had, in which he feigned to be angry and they to be
defiant. They jumped about just out of his reach, jeering at

him. "Old Father Smither!" they cried, as often as their peals
of laughter would let them cry anything at all. But it struck
me as very strange that their sing-song derision was not going
to the right tune and rhythm; for there is a genuine folk-tune
which I thought indissolubly wedded to this derisive formula.
Beginning in a long drawl, it throws all the weight on the first
and fourth syllables: "*Old* Father *Smith*-er." But these
children, apparently ignorant of it, had invented a rhythm of
their own, in which the first syllable, "Old," was almost elided,
and the weight was thrown on the next. I could not help
wondering at the breach which this indicated with the ancient
folk traditions.

If it were necessary, plentiful other evidence could be produced of the children's great need for more subjects upon which
to exercise their thoughts and fancies. For one example: some
years ago a little maidservant from this village was found, when
she went to her first "place" in the town, never to have seen
a lamb, or a pond of water. This was an extreme case, perhaps; but it suggests how badly the children are handicapped.
As recently as last year, when a circus was visiting the town, I
asked two village boys on the road if they had seen the procession. They had not; nor had they ever in their lives seen a
camel or an elephant; but one of them "thought he should
know an elephant, by his trunk." He was probably eight years
old; and it is worth noting that he must have owed his enlightenment to books or pictures seen at school; indeed, there is
nothing of the sort to be learnt at home, where there are no
books, and where the parents, themselves limited to so narrow
a range of experience and therefore of ideas, are not apt to
encourage inquisitiveness in their children. A man who lived
near me a few years ago could often be heard, on Sundays and
on summer evenings, chiding his little son for that fault.
"Don't you keep on astin' so many questions," was his formula,
which I must have heard dozens of times. One can sympa-
thize: it would be so much easier to give the child a bun, or

the cottage equivalent, and order him to eat it; but that does not satisfy the child's appetite for information. Probably the great difficulty is that the children's questions can hardly any longer turn upon these old-fashioned subjects which the parents understand, but upon new-fangled things. And, apart from all this, I suspect that in most of the cottages the old notion prevails that children should be kept in their place, and not encouraged to bother grown-up people with their trumpery affairs.

From the contrast between the talk of the village youngsters and that of children who are better cared for, I inferred just now a want of " flow " in the thoughts of the former, as though the little scrappy ideas existed in their brains without much relationship to one another. Of course it is possible that the brain activity is far greater than one would surmise, and that it only seems sluggish because of the insufficiency of our village speech as a means of expression, for certainly the people's vocabulary is extremely limited, while they have no habit of talking in sentences of any complexity. Yet where a language has neither abundant names for ideas, nor flexible forms of construction to exhibit variations of thought, it is hard to believe that the brain-life itself is anything but cramped and stiff.

And if the crude phrasing indicates poverty in the more definite kinds of ideas, I cannot help thinking that another feature of the children's talk betrays no less a poverty, in respect to those more vague ideas which relate to behaviour and to perception of other people's position and feelings. It was since beginning this chapter that I happened to be walking for some distance in front of four children—three girls and a boy— from a comfortable middle-class home. It was a Sunday morning, and they were chatting very quietly, so that their words did not reach me; but I found it very agreeable to hear the variety of cadence in their voices, with occasionally pauses, and then a resumption of easy talk, as if they had got a subject to consider in serious lights, and recognized each other's right to be heard and understood. Indeed, it bordered on priggishness, and perhaps over-stepped the border; but nevertheless it made me feel jealous for our village children, for in the conversation of village children one never hears that suggestion of a considerate mental attitude towards one another. The speech is without flexibility or modulation of tone; harsh, exclamatory, and screaming, or guttural and drawling. Rarely, if ever, does one derive from it an impression that the children are growing to regard one another's feelings, or one another's thoughts. A further point must be mentioned. I hinted that there might be an additional cause, besides physical privations, for the loss of the children's attractiveness in many cases even before they leave school. My belief is that, as they approach the age when ideas of a sensitive attitude towards life should begin to sway them, unconsciously moulding the still growing features into fineness, those ideas do not come their way. The boys of eight begin to look, at times, like little men; and the girls of eleven and upwards begin to show signs of acquaintance with struggling domestic economies; but neither boys nor girls discover, in the world into which they are growing up, any truly helpful ideas of what it is comely to be and to think. Lingering peasant notions of personal fitness and of integrity keep them from going viciously wrong, so that when they come to puberty their perplexed spirits are not without guidance; yet, after all, the peasant conditions are gone, and seeing that the new wage-earning conditions do not, of themselves, suggest worthy ideas of personal bearing, the children's faculties for that sort of thing soon cease to unfold, and with a gradual slackening of development the attractiveness disappears. The want is the more to be regretted in that, at a later time of life, when the women have been moulded by motherhood and the men by all the stress and responsibility of their position, such composure and strength often appear in them as to justify a suspicion that these uncared-for people are by nature amongst the very best of the English.

V

THE FORWARD MOVEMENT

XXI

THE FORWARD MOVEMENT

THE last twenty years having witnessed so much change in the village, it is interesting to speculate as to the farther changes that may be looked for in the years to come; indeed, it is more than merely interesting. Educational enthusiasts are busy; legislators have their eye on villages; throughout the leisured classes it is habitual to look upon " the poor " as a sort of raw material, to be remodelled according to leisured ideas of what is virtuous, or refined, or useful, or nice; and nobody seems to reflect that the poor may be steadily, albeit unconsciously, moving along a course of their own, in which they might be helped a little, or hindered a little, by outsiders, but from which they will not in the long run be turned aside. Yet such a movement, if it is really proceeding, will obviously stultify the most well-intentioned schemes that are not in accordance with it.

And, if I am not greatly mistaken, it is under way. That seems to me an ill-grounded complacency which permits easy-going people to say lightly, " Of course we want a few reforms," as if, once those reforms were brought to pass, the labouring population would thereafter settle down and change no more. In one respect, no doubt, there is little more to be looked for. The changes so far observed have been thrust upon the people from outside—changes in their material or social environment, followed by mere negations on their part, in the abandonment of traditional outlooks and ambitions; and of course in that negative direction the movement must come to an end at last. But when there are no more old habits to be given up, there is still plenty of scope for acquiring new ones, and this is the possibility that has to be considered. What if, quietly and out of sight—so quietly and inconspicuously as to be unnoticed even by the people themselves—their English nature, dissatisfied with negations, should have instinctively set to work in a positive direction to discover a new outlook and new ambitions? What if the merely mechanical change should have become transmuted into a vital growth in the people's spirit—a growth which, having life in it, must needs go on spontaneously by a process of self-unfolding? If that should be the case, as I am persuaded that it is, then the era of change in the village is by no means over; on the contrary, it is more likely that the greatest changes are yet to come.

As the signs which should herald their approach will be those of recovery from the mental and spiritual stagnation into which the village has been plunged, and as we may regard that stagnation as the starting-point from which any further advance will proceed, it is worth while to fix it in our minds by a similitude. What has most obviously happened to the village population resembles an eviction, when the inmates of a cottage have been turned out upon the road-side with their goods and chattels, and there they sit, watching the dismantling of their home, and aware only of being moved against their will. It is a genuine movement of them; yet it does not originate with them; and the first effect of it upon them is stagnation. Unable to go on in their old way, yet knowing no other way in which to go on, they merely wait disconsolate.

The similitude really fits the case very well, in this village at least, and probably in many others. Of the means whereby the people have been thrust out from the peasant traditions in which they were at home I have discussed only the chief one—namely, the enclosure of the common. That was the cause which irresistibly compelled the villagers to quit their old life; but of course there were other causes, less conspicuous here than they have been elsewhere, yet operative here too. Free Trade,

whilst it made the new thrift possible, at the same time effec-
tually undermined many of the old modes of earning a living;
and more destructive still has been the gradual adoption of
machinery for rural work. We are shocked to think of the
unenlightened peasants who broke up machines in the riots of
the eighteen-twenties, but we are only now beginning to see
fully what cruel havoc the victorious machines played with the
defeated peasants. Living men were " scrapped "; and not
only living men. What was really demolished in that struggle
was the country skill, the country lore, the country outlook; so
that now, though we have no smashed machinery, we have a
people in whom the pride of life is broken down : a shattered
section of the community; a living engine whose fly-wheel of
tradition is in fragments and will not revolve again. Let us
mark the finality of that destruction before going further.
Whatever prosperity may return to our country places, it will
not be on the old terms. The " few reforms," whether in the
direction of import duties, or small holdings, or " technical
education " in ploughing or fruit-pruning or forestry or sheep-
shearing, can never in themselves be a substitute for the lost
peasant traditions, because they are not the same kind of thing.
For those traditions were no institutions set up and cherished
by outside authority. Associated though they were with in-
dustrial and material well-being, they meant much more than
that to country folk; they lived in the popular tastes and habits,
and they passed on spontaneously from generation to generation, as a sort of rural civilization. And you cannot create that
sort of thing by Act of Parliament, or by juggling with tariffs,
or by school lessons. An imitation of the shell of it might be
set up; but the life of it is gone, not to be restored. That is
the truth of the matter. The old rural outlook of England is
dead; and the rural English, waiting for something to take its
place, for some new tradition to grow up amongst them, are in
a state of stagnation.

In looking for signs of new growth, it must be observed that not all steps in the transition are equally significant. Amongst the modifications of habit slowly proceeding in the village to-day, there are some which should be regarded rather as a final relinquishment of old ways than as a spontaneous forward movement into new ones. Thus, although the people comply more and more willingly with the by-laws of the sanitary authority, I could not say with conviction that this is anything more than a compliance. As they grow less used to squalor, no doubt they cannot bear its offensiveness so well as of old; but we may not infer from this fact that any new and positive aspirations towards a comelier home-life have been born in them. The improvement is only one of those negative changes that have been thrust upon them from outside.

Nor can anything better be said of their increasing conformity to the requirements of the new thrift. I think it true that the wages are spent more prudently than of old. The sight of a drunken man begins to be unusual; he who does not belong to a " club " is looked upon as an improvident fool; but to imagine the people thus parsimonious for the pleasure of it is to imagine a vain thing. Their occasional outbursts of extravagance and generosity go to show that their innermost taste has not found a suitable outlet in wage-earning economy. That miserly " thrift " which is preached to them as the whole duty of " the Poor "—what attractions can it have for their human nature? If men practise it, they do so under the compulsion of anxiety, of fear. Their acquiescence may seem like a change; yet as it springs from no germinating tastes or desires or inner initiative, so it acquires no true momentum. Not in that, nor in any other submissive adaptation to the needs of the passing moment, shall we see where the villagers are really rousing out of stagnation into a new mode of life.

On the other hand, where their vitality goes out, under no necessity, but of its own accord, to do something new just for the sake of doing it, there a true growth is proceeding; and there are signs that this is happening. Especially one notes three main directions in which, as I think, the village is astir—three directions, coinciding with three kinds of opportunity. The opportunities are those afforded, first by the Church and other agencies of a missionary kind; second, by newspapers; and third, by political agitation. In each of these directions the village instincts appear to be finding something that they want, and to be moving towards it spontaneously—for they are under no compulsion to move. The invitations from the Church, it is true, never cease; but no villager is obliged to accept them against his will, any more than a horse need drink water put before him.

1. In estimating the influence of the Church (Dissent has but a small following here) it should be remembered that until some time after the enclosure of the common the village held no place of worship of any denomination. Moreover, the comparatively few inhabitants of that time were free from interference by rich people or by resident employers. They had the valley to themselves; they had always lived as they liked, and been as rough as they liked; and there must have been memories amongst them—quite recent memories then—of the lawless life of other heath-dwellers, their near neighbours, in the wide waste hollows of Hindhead. We may therefore surmise that when the church was built a sprinkling at least of the villagers were none too well pleased. This may partly explain the sullen hostility of which the clergy are still the objects in certain quarters of the village, and which the Pharisaism of some of their friends does much to keep alive. The same causes may have something to do with the fact that the majority of the labouring men appear to take no interest at all in religion.

Still, there are more than a few young men, and of the old village stock too, who yield very readily to the influences of the Church. A family tradition no doubt predisposes them to do so; for, be it said, not all of the old villagers were irreligious. Echoes of a rustic Christianity, gentle and resigned as that which the Vicar of Wakefield taught to his flock, may be heard to-day in the talk of aged men and women here and there; and though that piety has gone rather out of fashion, the taste for something like it survives in these young men. The Church attracts them: they approve its ideas of decorous life; it is a school of good manners to them, if not of high thinking, with the result that they begin to be quite a different sort of people from their fathers and grandfathers. A pleasant suavity and gentleness marks their behaviour. They are greatly self-respecting. Their tendency is to adopt and live up to the middle-class code of respectability.

Neither by temperament nor by outlook are they equipped for the hardship of real labouring life. These are the men, rather, who get the lighter work required by the residential people in the villa gardens; or they fill odd places in the town, where character is wanted more than strength or skill. They fill them well, too, in very trustworthy and industrious fashion. A few of them have learnt trades, and are saving money, as bricklayers, carpenters, clerks even. It was from the ranks of this group that a young man emerged, some years ago, as a speculating builder. He put up three or four cottages, and then came to grief; but I never heard that anybody but himself suffered loss by the collapse of his venture. He has left the neighbourhood, and I mention him now only to exhibit the middle-class tendencies of his kind. You will not find any of these men going to a public house. The " Institute " caters for them, with its decorous amusements—billiards, dominoes, crib-bage; but they do not much affect the Institute Reading Room; indeed, I believe them to be intellectually very docile to authority. Opinions they have, on questions of the day, but not opinions formed by much effort of their own. The need of the village, as they have felt it, is less for mental than for ethical help. They desire something to guide their conduct and their pastimes, and this leads them to respond to the invitation of the Church and its allied influences.

I have an impression, too, that indirectly, through their example, others are affected by those influences who do not so consciously yield to them; at any rate a softening of manners seems to be in progress in the village. It is not much, perhaps; it is certainly very indefinite, and no doubt there are other causes helping to further it; but, such as it is, the chief credit for it is due to the lead given by the Church. Indeed, no other agency has done anything at all in the way of proposing to the people an art of living, a civilization, to replace that of the old rustic days.

2. With few exceptions the newspapers—chiefly weeklies, but here and there a daily—which come into the villagers' hands are of the " yellow press " kind; but for once a good effect may be attributed to them. It resembles that which, in a smaller way, springs from the opportunities of travelling afforded by railways. Just as few of our people now are wholly restricted in their ideas of the world to this valley and the horizons visible from its sides, but the most of them, in excursion holidays at least, have seen a little of the extent and variety of England, so, thanks to the cheap press, ideas and information about the whole world are finding their way into the cottages of the valley; and at the present stage it is not greatly important that the information is less trustworthy than it might be. The main thing is that the village mind should stretch itself, and look beyond the village; and this is certainly happening. The mere material of thought, the quantity of subjects in which curiosity may take an interest, is immeasurably greater than it was even twenty years ago; and, if but sleepily as yet, still the curiosity of the villagers begins to wake up. However superior you may think yourself, you must not now approach any of the younger labouring men in the assumption that they have not heard of the subject you speak of. The coal-heaver, whose poverty of ideas I described farther back, was talking to me (after that chapter was written) about the life of coal-miners. He told of the poor wages they get for their dangerous work; he discoursed

of mining royalties, and explained some points as to freightage and railway charges; and he was drifting towards the subject of Trades Unions when our short walk home together came to an end. Of course in this case the man's calling had given a direction to his curiosity; but there are many subjects upon which the whole village may be supposed to be getting ideas. Shackleton and the South Pole are probably household words in most of the cottages; it may be taken for granted that the wonders of flying machines are being eagerly watched; it must not be taken for granted at all that the villagers are ignorant about disease germs, and the causes of consumption, and the spreading of plague by rats. Long after the King's visit to India, ideas of Indian scenes will linger in the valley; and presently, when the Panama Canal nears completion, and pictures of it begin to be given in the papers, there will hardly be a labourer but is more or less familiar with the main features of the work, and is more or less aware of its immense political and commercial importance.

Thus the field of vision opens out vastly, ideas coming into it in enough variety and abundance to begin throwing side-lights upon one another and to illumine the whole village outlook upon life. And while the field widens, the people are winning their way to a greater power of surveying it intelligently; for one must notice how the newspapers, besides giving information, encourage an acceptance of non-parochial views. The reader of them is taken into the public confidence. Instead of a narrow village tradition, national opinions are at his disposal, and he is helped to see, as it were from the outside, the general aspect of questions which, but for the papers, he would only know by his individual experience from the inside. To give one illustration: the labourer out of work understands now more than his own particular misfortunes from that cause. He is discovering that unemployment is a world-wide evil, which spreads like an infectious disease, and may be treated accordingly. It is no small change to note, for in such ways, all unawares, the people fall into the momentous habit of thinking about abstract ideas which would have been beyond the range of their forefathers' intellectual power; and with the ideas, their sentiments gain in dignity, because the newspapers, with whatever ulterior purpose, still make their appeal to high motives of justice, or public spirit, or public duty. Fed on this fare, a national or standardized sentiment is growing amongst the villagers, in place of the local prejudices which, in earlier times, varied from valley to valley and allowed the people of one village occasionally to look upon those in the next as their natural enemies.

3. Once or twice before I have mentioned, as characteristic of the peasant outlook, the fatalism which allowed the poor to accept their position as part of the unalterable scheme of the universe, and I associated the attitude with their general failure to think in terms of cause and effect. It would seem that this settled state of mind is slowly giving way under the political excitement of the last ten years. I cannot say, as yet, that anything worthy to be called hope has dawned upon the cottagers; but an inclination to look into things for themselves is discernible.

The change, such as it is, was begun—or, let us say, the ground was prepared for its beginning—by the distress of unemployment which followed the South African War; for then was bred that great discontent which came to the surface at last in the General Election of 1906. I well remember how, on the day when the Liberal victory in this division was made known, the labouring men, standing about with nothing to do, gladdened at the prospects of the relief which they supposed must at once follow, and how their hungry eyes sparkled with excitement. "Time there *was* a change," one of them said to me, "with so many o' we poor chaps out o' work." Then, as the months went by, and things worsened rather than bettered, reaction set in. "'Twas bad enough under the Conservatives, but 'tis ten times worse under the Liberals." That was the opinion I heard expressed, often enough to suggest that it was passing into a by-word. So, to all appearance, the old apathy was falling upon the people, as no doubt it had often done before after a momentary gleam of hope, confirming them in the belief that, whatever happened, it would not, as they said, "make much odds to the likes o' we."

This time, however, a new factor in the situation had been introduced, which tended to keep alive in village minds the possibility that Poverty, instead of being the act of God, was an effect of causes which might be removed. The gospel of "Tariff Reform" promised so much as to make it worth the people's while to pay a little attention to politics. Men who had never before in their lives tried to follow a logical argument began at last to store up in their memory reasons and figures in support of the fascinating doctrine, and if they were puzzle-headed over it, they were not more so than their leaders. Besides, in their case merely to have begun is much. Look at the situation. During six or seven years, there has been before the village a vision of better times to be realized by political action, and by support of a programme or a policy, and the interest which the people have taken in it marks a definite step forwards from the lethargy of stagnation in which they had previously been sunk. True, this particular vision seems fading now. Just when it ought to have been growing clearer and nearer, if it was to justify itself, it becomes dim and remote, and my neighbours, I fancy, are reverting to their customary attitude of aloofness from party politics; but I should be much surprised to find that it is quite in the old spirit. For the old spirit was one of indifference; it rested on the persuasion that politicians of either side were only seeking their own ends, and that the game was a rich man's game, in which the poor were not meant to share. That, however, is hardly the persuasion now. If the labourers hold aloof, keeping their own counsel, it is no longer as outsiders, but as interested watchers, ready to take part

strongly whenever a programme shall be put before them that
deserves their help.

I have suggested that the tendency of those who are in-
fluenced by the Church is towards a middle-class outlook, and
that their interest centres in developments of taste and conduct
rather than of intellect and opinion. Nothing so definite can
be said as to the effects of newspaper reading and political
excitement; nevertheless, I am conscious of effects everywhere
present. The labourers whose interests turn in this direction
seem to be treading in the footsteps of the skilled artisans in
the town, towards ambitions not in all respects identical with
those of the middle-classes. Of course the unskilled labourer
earning eighteen shillings a week has not equal opportunities
with the man who earns thirty-six; he cannot buy the newspapers and occasional books to which the other treats himself
and his children, and in general he is less well informed. But
the same grave and circumspect talk goes down with the one as
with the other; to both the same topics are interesting.

And for me the probability of a development for our village
labourers similar to that of the town artisans is heightened by
recollection of what artisans themselves were like, say a quarter
of a century ago. I knew a few of these very well. As craftsmen they were as able as those of to-day; but their crafts had
not taught them to think. While they worked by rule of
thumb, outside their work they were as full of prejudices, and
as unable to grasp reasons, as any of my village neighbours.
The most of them, in fact, had been born in villages near the
town, and retained a good deal of the rural outlook. Their
gardens, and the harvest—yes, and odd scraps of very ancient
folk-lore which they still believed—occupied an important place
in their attention. They had quite the old attitude towards
their employers; quite the old stubborn distrust of innovations
in their work. When, however, you turn to their successors,
you find a difference. I will not say that they are less able than

their predecessors, or less trustworthy; but they have broken away from all that old simplicity of mind; they are thinking for themselves, and informing themselves, with an unresting and unhasting interest, about what the rest of the world knows. It fills me with shame, when I consider my own so much better opportunities, to find how much these hard-working men have learnt, and with what cool tenacity they think. Where they are most wanting is in enthusiasm and the hopes that breed it; or say, in belief that the world may yet change for the better—though here, too, political excitement is doing its fateful work. I find them very jealous for their children to do well: free education has not sapped their sense of parental responsibility, but has inspired them with ambitions, though not for themselves. For themselves they are conscious of a want of that book-learned culture which the practice of their skilled crafts cannot bestow, and this makes them suspicious of those who have it and diffident in conversation with them. But underneath this reticence and willingness to hear dwells a quiet scepticism which has no docility in it, and is not to be persuaded out of its way by any eloquence or any emotion. Missionary influences, like those of church and chapel, make but little impression on these quiet-eyed men. The tendency is towards a scientific rather than an aesthetic outlook.

And just as, amongst the skilled craftsmen, there are individuals representing every stage of the advance from five-and-twenty years ago until now, so the earlier stages at least of the same advance are represented, one beyond another, by labouring men in this village. I could not find any labourers who are so far forward as the forwardest artisans; but I could find some who have travelled, say, half the way, and many who have reached different points between that and the stagnation which was the starting-point for all. Hence I cannot doubt that the villagers in general are moving on the route along which the town artisans have passed a generation ahead of them. They are hindered by great poverty; hampered by the excessive fatigues of their daily work; entrammelled by remnants of the peasant traditions which still cling about them; but the movement has begun. The first stupefying effect of their eviction from the peasant life is passing away, and they are setting their faces towards the future, to find a new way of life.

It may be urged that, along with the Church, the newspaper and politics, education should have been named, as a fourth power affecting the village destinies. A moment's consideration, however, will discover that it does not come into the same category with those three influences, if only for this reason, that it is forced upon the village children from outside, while the older people have no chance to interest themselves in it as they have in the Church teachings or in the daily paper. No spontaneous movement, therefore, such as I have outlined in the other cases, can be traced in regard to education; but I had a stronger reason than that for omitting mention of it. To be quite plain, I do not think it is making anything like so much impression on the village life as it ought to make, and as it is commonly supposed to be making. It is not quite a failure; but it is by no means a great success. In so far as it has enabled the people to read their papers (and it has not done that very well) it has been serviceable; but neither as a cause of change nor as a guide into happier ways of life has it any claim to especial mention in these chapters. I am not saying that it is unworthy of attention: on the contrary, there is no subject relating to the village that demands so much. If, as I believe, it is one, and the foremost, of those activities which are largely abortive because they have not got into touch with the spontaneous movement of the village life, the matter is of the utmost seriousness. But this is not the place for entering into it; for I have not set out to criticize the varied experiments in reform which are being tried upon the labouring people. My book is finished, now that I have pointed to the inner changes going on in the village itself.

As to the future of those changes, I will not add to what I have already said, but there is evidently much room for speculation; and those who best know the villagers—their brave patience, their sincerity, the excellent groundwork of their nature—and those who see how full of promise are the children, generation after generation, until hardship and neglect spoil them, will be slow to believe what leisured folk are so fond of saying—namely, that these lowly people owe their lowliness to defects in their inborn character. It is too unlikely. The race which, years ago, in sequestered villages, unaided by the outer world at all, and solely by force of its own accumulated traditions, could build up that sturdy peasant civilization which has now gone—that race, I say, is not a race naturally deficient. There is no saying what its offspring may not achieve, once they get their powers of intellect awake on modern lines and can draw freely upon the great world for ideas.

At any rate, the hope is great enough to forbid the indulgence of any deep regret for what has gone by. The old system had gone on long enough. For generations the villagers had grown up and lived and died with large tracts of their English vitality neglected, unexplored; and I do not think the end of that wasteful system can be lamented by anyone who believes in the English. Rather it should reconcile us to the disillusionments of this present time of transition. They are devastating, I admit; for me, they have spoilt a great deal of that pleasure which the English country used to give me, when I still fancied it to be the scene of a joyful and comely art of living. I know now that the landscape is not peopled by a comfortable folk, whose dear and intimate love of it gave a human interest to every feature of its beauty; I know that those who live there have in fact lost touch with its venerable meanings, while all their existence has turned sordid and anxious and worried; and knowing this, I feel a forlornness in country places, as if all their best significance were gone. But, notwithstanding this, I would not go back. I would not lift a finger, or say a word, to restore the past time, for fear lest in doing so I might be retarding a movement which, when I can put these sentiments aside, looks like the prelude to a renaissance of the English country-folk.

NOTE.—In the preceding chapters no reference is made either to the new Insurance Act or to recent labour unrest. The book was, in fact, already in the publishers' hands when those matters began to excite general attention; and it hardly seems necessary now, merely for the sake of being momentarily up to date, to begin introducing allusions which after all would leave the main argument unchanged.

December, 1911.

THE END